beading

THE POTTER NEEDLEWORK LIBRARY

beading

Diana Vernon

Photography by Linda Burgess

Clarkson Potter/Publishers
New York

page 2: Fringed Bag (see page 57)
page 3: Beaded Cuff links (see page 42)

Detail photography · Peter Cassidy, Dave King
Illustrations · Tim Pearce
Technical drawings · Stephen Dew

Published by Clarkson N. Potter/Publishers, 201 East 50th Street, New York, NY 10022. Member of the Crown Publishing Group.

Random House, Inc. New York, Toronto, London, Sydney, Auckland

CLARKSON N. POTTER, POTTER, and colophon are trademarks of Clarkson N. Potter, Inc.

Originally published in Great Britain by Quadrille Publishing Limited in 1995.

Manufactured in Hong Kong.

Library of Congress Cataloging-in-Publication data is available upon request.

ISBN 0-517-88468-2

10 9 8 7 6 5 4 3 2 1

First American Edition

contents

Introduction

The allure of beads in all their myriad shapes, sizes, and colors has captivated our aesthetic and tactile senses since prehistoric peoples first threaded bones and shells onto thongs and animal sinews to adorn their bodies.

For many centuries, beads have been used as a focus for prayer and contemplation, as with the string of prayer beads used by Hindus and Buddhists and the rosary used by Christian worshippers. Many other religions also use some form of prayer beads – the word "bead" itself is thought to be derived from the Old English gebed or bedu and the Middle English bede, all of which mean prayer. Even without a spiritual focus, many a person seeking calm has fiddled with their pearls or string of "worry beads"!

The earliest beads were made from clay, stone, shells (such as the wampum made and used by Native Americans) and semiprecious stones. The Egyptians developed a special clay recipe called "faience," or Egyptian paste, and the beads created by this process were worked into the collars worn by the Pharoahs. Beads are depicted in wall paintings and discovered in the pyramids.

It is believed that one of the first applications of glassmaking was in the manufacture of glass beads. These were produced in such quantities that they became an important item for trade and developed into a worldwide currency. These beads became known as "trade-wind" or "pony" beads, and the beading of Native American and African nations preserved from this time demonstrates the artistry and skill with which they were worked.

Before this, medieval embroiderers in Europe had been incorporating drilled pearls, coral, and semiprecious gemstones into their work. Later, during the sixteenth and seventeenth centuries, glass beads and pearls were used in great abundance to decorate embroidery and costume. Then in the mid-nineteenth century the Victorians in England developed a real passion for decorating items of interior furnishing with beading. This enthusiasm was no doubt fuelled by the repeal of the British Glass Tax in 1845 which made glass affordable.

This book aims to demonstrate the glory of beads through technique and practical application and to continue a tradition enjoyed since time immemorial.

Starting to bead

Beading is an age-old technique and an exciting, visual and tactile craft. This book deals mainly with beading using a needle and thread, perhaps the easiest form of beading of all. With no major equipment to worry about, it is a craft that is easily portable: if you are pressed for time, your design can be picked up, carried with you and worked at your convenience.

Some of the projects in this book are so easy that a young child could make them; others are more complex and involve careful charting. Once you have mastered the basic techniques, such as a beaded triangle for a bookmark or a picot drop for a pillow edging, you might well feel inspired to create something more ambitious – a beaded curtain or wall hanging perhaps. This chapter presents some simple but effective projects for needlewoven beading.

the beads

Naming and describing beads can be problematic. The same bead may go by different names in different places, and bead sellers may call beads that appear quite similar by a variety of names. Often, bead names are derived from the trade names used for so long that their origins, especially if they have been abbreviated over the years, are no longer known. One example is the beautiful iridescent metallic beads now called "3 cut" due to their 3-cut, faceted exterior, which was formerly known as "lofo" or "Kashmir" – though no one knows why. And a bead importer may fail to record the origin of a particular bead name, making such information hard to trace once the merchant has retired.

Rocailles

Two commonly used small beads are "rocailles" and "seed beads." Technically, a rocaille is oblate – that is, a sphere flattened at its poles – while a seed bead is completely round. ("Rocaille" is a French word meaning "little rock," and an architectural *style rocaille*, which later became rococo – based on rounded lines, such as rocks and shells – was in fashion during the reign of Louis XV.)

Many bead sellers now describe all small glass beads, including seed beads, as rocailles, since most are not completely spherical or round. However, aware of the confusion, some bead catalogs now list only "small glass beads" rather than referring to rocailles or seed beads, so these terms might disappear in due course.

Old trade names you may come across include Tosca, faceted on the outside, with a square hole; Charlotte, faceted on the outside, with a round hole; Pompadour, larger, with a large hole (traditional for lace bobbins); Pound, rocailles once sold by weight; 3 cut, with 3 cuts or facets on the outside; and 2 cut (2 cuts or facets on the outside).

Opaque
These are of one solid color and may have a polished, matt, or chalky finish.

Transparent
There are four different varieties of transparent rocailles:
Plain transparent.
Color-lined transparent, where a pale color or clear bead is lined with a second color, thus producing an attractive bicolored effect.

Silver-lined transparent, where the bead is lined with silver and usually has a square-cut hole to reflect the silver with greater intensity.

Transparent with iridescent finish, usually called "iris" and sometimes "rainbow" or "ab," the latter an abbreviation of "aurora borealis."

Pearlized
These have a pearly finish to the glass, not a pearl "skin" (see Pearls, below).

Luster
These rocailles have a high, often metallic, gloss finish.

Metallic As the name suggests, these rocailles have a metallic finish.

Bugles

Bugles are glass tubes mainly available in sizes 2mm to 30mm. There are three profiles: round with a round hole, round with a square hole, and faceted with a round hole. The finishes available are similar to those for rocailles.

Pearls

Artificial
Artificial pearls are available in round, seed, baroque, and fancy shapes (usually flower and leaf). They come in white, ivory, and pastel shades, as well as gold and silver. The pearl finish is a "skin" of varnish and the beads should be handled carefully.

Mother-of-pearl
This variety of pearl is formed from oyster shells.

Natural
Natural pearls are available in round and "baroque" (irregular) shapes. They are, however, very expensive, so allow for this in your design budget.

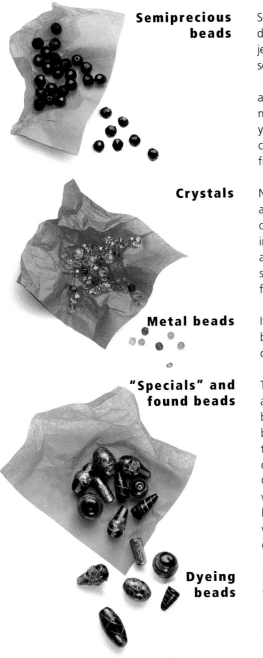

Semiprecious beads

Some semiprecious stones are easier to drill than others: garnet, quartz, amber, jet, moonstone, coral, and jade are some of those most often used.

Jet, the fossilized mineral, is very soft and brittle and is therefore not an ideal material for beads as it can shatter. If you see "jet" beads described in a catalog, they are most likely to be made from black glass and manganese. (This combination is often called "French jet," possibly from the word *jais*, the French for jet, which is the term embroiderers' once used to describe beads in general – in a seventeenth-century book by the embroiderer Charles Saint Aubin, he describes bead embroidery as *La Broderie en Jais*.) However, if the "jet" is warm to the touch, the beads may well be real jet.

Crystals

Natural crystal quartz beads are available, but the term usually refers to cut-glass beads and drops. These come in a variety of shapes and cuts of facet, and in many beautiful colors. Often, some of the facets will be mirror finished to increase the sparkle effect, while the shapes available include "marguerites" (daisy shapes) and hearts.

Other crystals which can be incorporated with beading are "loc rosen", which are embroidery stones with a flat back, faceted surface, and central hole.

Metal beads

It is possible to buy gold and silver beads, which are often plated. Brass, copper, and other metal beads are also available and can be very effective, but it is wise to consider whether they will tarnish or be too heavy for the thread.

"Specials" and found beads

There are many beautiful beads available, including handblown glass beads, Venetian glass, and lampwork beads (where trails of molten glass are trickled around a bead or flower, or dot designs are formed). There are also Chinese lacquer, Japanese magatama, which are rocailles with an off-center hole, and beads made from perfumed wax – a good book on potpourri will explain how. It is worth hunting for specials at antique fairs and in bric-à-brac shops. Look through old jewelry and button boxes, too: many a broken necklace has been relegated to the button box and you may find a real treasure. You will also find beads made from clay, wood, paper, and plastics, as well as from natural objects such as seeds, nuts, bamboo, and shells. You can drill your own found objects using a fine modelmaker's drill to make beads.

Dyeing beads

It is possible to dye some small glass beads and pearls. Bead vendors will dye beads for you if you need a large quantity, but for small amounts it is easy to do yourself. Experiment to see how the different types take the dye.

You will need
French enamel varnish (FEV)
Methyl alcohol (thinner)
Small bowl or jam jar
Beads
Pencil or chopstick
White tissue paper

1 Mix one part FEV with two parts methyl alcohol in a jar or bowl. These proportions are approximate; for some beads, you may need more varnish.

2 If the beads are not pre-strung, string them onto a thread, submerge them in the mixture and swish around.
3 Using the end of a pencil or chopstick, lift the beads carefully out of the dye. Lay them on a piece of tissue paper and gently pat off the excess dye, then hang up to dry naturally.
NB If dyeing pearls, lift them from the dye, and then hang up immediately to dry. Do not pat dry, as the pearl varnish "skin" may become damaged.

other equipment

Most beading techniques involve very little in the way of tools and materials, but here are some basic guidelines to help you get started. Beading need not be an expensive craft – many of these materials you might find you already have at home.

The current interest in beads and beading is reflected in the expanding number of specialist bead shops and mail-order bead companies. Unusual and interesting beads have never been more widely available.

Working board

You will need a board on which to pin out flat needlewoven beading and fringe while it is being worked. A piece of cork board, or the fiberboard often known as macramé board, is ideal, although a thick cork tile or piece of foamcore will work just as well so long as it provides a firm surface.

If leaving work pinned to a board for any length of time, it is advisable to cover it with a piece of cloth or tissue paper to keep it dust free.

Needles

Beading needles are available in several sizes, but being very long and fine they tend to bend and break easily. You may find the finer sizes of milliner's (or "straw") needles (for example sizes 8 and 9) more reliable.

It is possible to make your own needles by bending a piece of fine wire, such as electrical fuse wire, and twisting the ends together to form an "eye" of whatever size you require, but this only works well with larger beads. Using the wire bent double and not twisted, but held tightly together in the fingers, is sometimes a successful method.

There are no hard-and-fast rules for selecting appropriate needles, so it is best to experiment. Try the particular bead hole on the needle, remembering to allow for the thickness of the thread used and the fact that a bead will usually have a needle passed through it twice during needleweaving – this means that the hole must be able to accommodate four thicknesses of the thread used.

Threads

There are many fine yet strong threads now available, but polyester thread, for example, is one that is particularly useful for beading.

Test the strength of a thread by trying to break it by pulling tightly. Synthetic fishing line and some nylon threads are strong, but are hard to control while working as they are quite springy. Waxed linen carpet thread and buttonhole thread are good for threading beads for fringe if they have large enough holes.

Running a thread over a block of beeswax will increase its tensile strength, and is useful when threading bugles and some faceted beads, as they tend to have very sharp edges. With beads with smaller holes, there can be disadvantages in that the wax is scraped off the thread as it passes through the bead hole and gathers between the beads, smearing the finished beadwork. Again, it is best to experiment to discover the methods that work well in each instance.

Wire

For the wire beading projects in this book (see Pin and Wire Beading chapter), you can use electrical (tinned copper) fuse wire. Wires with diameters of 0.345mm and 0.213mm are useful for small beads. Gold, silver, and some beautiful rainbow colors are to be found in fishing fly-tying wire.

Containers

It is helpful to store your beads in clear glass jars. For small quantities, little individual jam jars are good, while fishing-tackle boxes and the small partitioned boxes used for screws, nails, and so on are ideal for storing crystals and other specials (see page 11).

Transfer all of the beads you are using to shallow dishes or saucers. The little china dishes used by artists for mixing watercolor paint, or the plastic palettes sectioned into different-sized areas that are used for Chinese brush painting, are both excellent for this. Whatever you use, be sure that there is enough space in the dish to allow you to pick up each bead easily with the tip of the needle.

A piece of corrugated cardboard is useful for laying down a row of beads to see if you are happy with the overall effect; there are also bead-stringing boards available that are designed specifically for this purpose.

Other useful tools

All-metal scissors
These are useful for breaking off a particular bead – perhaps because it is cracked or chipped – from a strung thread without needing to unthread all the beads.

Tweezers
Tweezers are helpful in selecting a particular bead from a mixed pack.

Double-sided tape
This can be stuck onto your working surface and used to secure beads, needles, and pins ready for use.

Thimble
Special thimbles are available with a sticky, textured surface (similar to banknote-counting thimbles) that enables you to pick up beads without dropping them.

Glass-headed pins
Colored glass-headed pins can be used to mark particular sequences of threading and to count the number of beads in a row or round. To use in this way, slip the pin through the hole in the threaded bead.

Jeweler's pliers
Cut small pieces of felt and glue them to the jaws of these small pliers, so that if you need to coax a needle through a bead you can do so without scratching the surface of the needle. Use very carefully, as too much pressure could result in a cracked bead.

Handy hints
• If the beads you have bought are pre-strung, as they are for tambour bead embroidery (a method of attaching beads to fabric with a small hook), it is helpful to keep them on the string and transfer them onto the needle straight from it, especially if you are using a number of the same beads.
• If you need a number of the same color bead from loose beads – for instance, if you are making a length of fringe – instead of trying to locate each bead hole individually with the needle, use the following method. Pour the beads into a deep dish (a wooden salad bowl is ideal), thread a needle, and bouncing the bowl gently on your knees, plunge the needle rhythmically in and out of the bowl: the beads will jump onto the needle without your having to steer it tediously through each individual hole. This is the traditional method used in Venice by the bead threaders, who used the technique while holding 20 or more needles fanned out in their hands. Try it – it does work!

needlewoven beading

This is a method of interlacing beads with a needle and one length of thread. It is an extremely versatile technique that can be used for creating flat, one-dimensional objects, or shaped, three-dimensional items. Because this technique forms a structure of beads placed between beads, rather than on top of each other as in loomwoven beading, it is sometimes described as diagonal beadweaving due to the way the positioning of the beads lends itself to diagonal patterns. You can use this to advantage in your choice of color schemes. For information on how to chart a design see pages 98–99.

Starting off

This is the basic technique, but by varying the numbers of beads in rows, and changing the threading sequence, it is possible to create different effects: you will be shown how to work these in later chapters.

1 Make a "base" row of beads, either by stitching the beads onto a piece of fabric, or by stringing them out on a corkboard between two securing pins – one at each end – to hold the "base" or 1st row.
2 Pass needle and thread through 1st bead of 1st row, then thread a loose single bead and pass needle and thread through next bead of 1st row, adjacent to the one you have just gone through.
3 In effect you are hanging each bead of 2nd row between pairs of beads of 1st row. The edge bead hangs in alternate rows (see the colored bead in fig 1).
4 The 3rd row of beads will hang between pairs of beads of 2nd row, and so on (fig 2), continuing the sequence as in 1st two rows.

fig 1

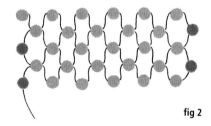

fig 2

Openwork beading

By threading more than one bead onto your needle, and passing the needle and thread through, for instance, every other pair of beads of the previous row, you can create openwork, lace, and honeycomb effects. By combining this method with simple beaded drops, you can work a variety of interesting decorative trimmings.

Also, by careful shaping of the structure, by increasing and decreasing the number and/or size of the beads used, a three-dimensional effect can be achieved.

Beaded triangle finish

If you decrease each row by one bead, you will create a triangular shape which, when finished off with a drop, makes an interesting trimming, or edging when repeated. This is the method used to embellish the pillow on page 21. It is equally effective when used singly, as shown opposite in the beaded bookmark.

Bead picot finish

fig 3   fig 4

The simplest way to attach a drop or to finish a string of bead fringe is to use a single bead (fig 3), by threading on a larger drop after the last bead of the work, or, for a fringed item, threading on a small bead (the "anchor" bead), and passing the needle up through the drop or the last bead of the fringe.

The bead picot finish is used to give an added richness to the beaded drop (fig 4) by threading on 4 beads and passing the needle through the first bead threaded of the 4. When the thread is pulled up firmly the 3 beads will form a "picot."

Beaded bookmark

You will need

14" (35cm) moiré ribbon, 2" (5cm)
  wide
1¼yd (1m) polyester thread
Needle fine enough to pass through
beads twice when threaded
39 iridescent blue beads (iri bl bd)
21 large gold rocailles (lg gld roc)
1 drop bead

To make

1 Lightly draw a line in soft pencil onto back of ribbon, about 2" (5cm) from end, and stitch 10 iri bl bd to ribbon width from right to left on right side, using reverse side line as a guide.
2 Turn under 2" (5cm) at beginning of ribbon and pin wrong sides together.
3 Continue to work beading following chart (fig 1), i.e. 2nd row, working left to right, pass needle back through 1st bead stitched (A) to ribbon on 1st row and begin to interlace beads to this base row as follows: 2 iri bl bd, 1 lg gld roc, 3 iri bl bd, 1 lg gld roc, 2 iri bl bd; then pass needle back through 1st bead (B) threaded to begin to work 3rd row.
4 When you have worked to single iri bl bd at row 10, thread 1 lg gld roc, 1 drop bead, 1 iri bl bd, 3 lge gld roc; pass needle up through the iri bl bd, drop bead, and lg gld roc and work a fastening-off stitch to secure (see below). Thread back down through beads and cut off neatly.
5 Turn under ribbon to form a hem and hand stitch down, neatly repeating this turned under and stitched hem at top of bookmark.
6 Cover carefully with layers of tissue paper or a pressing cloth and press with a cool iron, avoiding beading at the bottom edge.

This shows the principle of a fastening-off stitch. Pass needle under thread, forming a loop below the bead thread. Take needle over top of bead thread into loop. Pull very tightly.

The same stitch is used as a concealed fastening-on stitch by making a small stitch under fabric to create a loop, or passing needle and thread through some beads to conceal tail of thread.

The fastening-off stitch shown here applied to a string of beads.

fig 1

beaded trimmings

Beaded trimmings can give a rich, decorative effect to a variety of interior and fashion-related projects. Designing simple trimmings gives an opportunity to study the different effects that can be created by varying the color palette, the number and sizes of beads, and the threading sequence. Experimenting with different combinations of these elements will enable you to design more elaborate and visually interesting beadwork.

All three of the pillows that follow are trimmed on two opposite edges, so the bead quantities given here reflect this.

Wine silk pillow

You will need

16" (40cm) square pillow
Polyester thread
Needle fine enough to pass through beads twice when threaded
280 iridescent amber rocailles (iri amb roc)
140 8mm pink bugles (8m pk bg)
132 crimson rocailles (crm roc)
84 orange rocailles (org roc)
82 large gold rocailles (lg gld roc)
54 large crimson rocailles (lg crm roc)
42 purple barrel-shaped beads (pur b-s bd)
40 4mm-diam garnet beads (4m gnt bd)
22 8mm amethyst bugles (8m ame bg)
22 6mm-diam yellow crystals (6m yel crs)
20 6mm-diam amethyst crystals (6m ame crs)
20 6mm brown bugles (6m br bg)
12 8mm-diam dark amethyst faceted crystals (8m dk ame fc crs)
11 5mm-diam amber beads (5m amb bd)
10 8mm-diam dark amber faceted crystals (8m dk amb fc crs)
10 5mm-diam garnet beads (5m gnt bd)

To make up

1 Using pins as markers, measure one edge and at center point push in a pin vertically to mark it. Working from this center point, to both left and right of it mark each ¾" (2cm) point. You will then have a total of 21 pins to be used as markers.

2 Starting at either left or right side seam line, begin to work edging. Note that the following instructions assume that you are working from left to right.

3 Working long drop Thread 1 lg crm roc, 1 5m amb bd, 1 lg gld roc, 1 pur b-s bd, 1 org roc, 1 8m ame bg, 1 crm roc, 1 6m yel crs, 1 lg crm roc, 1 8m dk ame fc crs, 1 org roc; then pass needle up through all beads threaded before last org roc. This will then form the long drop. Pull thread to ensure that drop hangs straight and make a small fastening-off stitch to secure. Thread your needle invisibly through seam stitching and then advance one bead width to the right.

fig 1

4 Working in-between beading Thread 1 iri amb roc, 1 crm roc, 1 8m pk bg, 1 lg gld roc, 1 4m gnt bd, 3 iri amb roc; then pass needle up through l 4m gnt bd and lg gld roc. This will form a picot of the 3 iri amb roc. Thread 1 8m pk bg, 1crm roc, 1 iri amb roc. Now stitch into seam line one bead width to left of next pin marker, and make a small fastening-off stitch to secure. Now thread needle invisibly through seam line, emerging again at next pin marker.

5 Working shorter drop Thread 1 lg gld roc, 1 pur b-s bd, 1 org roc, 1 6m br bg, 1 lg crm roc, 1 8m pk bg, 1 org roc, 1 6m ame crs, 1 crm roc; then pass needle up through all beads threaded before last crm roc. This will form the shorter drop and there will be 10 of these in total. Pull thread so that drop hangs straight and make a small fastening-off stitch to secure. Again advance invisibly through seam line, one bead width to the right, to repeat previous bead threading sequence, which is repeated

17

between each drop (fig 1).

6 Working second long drop Thread 1 org roc, 1 5m gnt bd, 1 lg gld roc, 1 pur b-s bd, 1 org roc, 1 8m ame bg, 1 crm roc, 1 8m dk amb fc crs, 1 crm roc; then pass needle up through all beads before last crm roc and continue as for 1st long drop.

7 Continue working in-between beading, short drop (all identical), in-between beading, 1st long drop, and so on. The trimming will be as illustrated (fig 2).

fig 2

8 The finishing step To give a continuous beaded effect along seam line of pillow, between each "between the drops" beading sequence, thread 1 iri amb roc, 1 8m pk bg, 1 iri amb roc, and stitch down, threading invisibly along seam line to the next point "between the drops" (fig 3).

9 Repeat all instructions given above to work beaded edging on opposite side of pillow.

fig 3

Gold silk pillow

You will need

16" (40cm) square pillow
32" (80cm) bronze or gold metallic ribbon, 2" (5cm) wide
Gold metallic thread, polyester thread
Needle fine enough to pass through beads twice when threaded
240 iridescent gold rocailles (iri gld roc)
40 iridescent amber rocailles (iri amb roc)
36 orange rocailles (org roc)
26 5mm-diam bronze faceted beads (5m brz fc bd)
22 large gold rocailles (lg gld roc)
14 5mm-diam amber beads (5m amb bd)
10 1cm-diam yellow crystals (1cm yel crs)
8 8mm-diam amber faceted beads (8m amb fc bd)
6 bronze rocailles (brz roc)
4 6mm-diam amber faceted beads (6m amb fc bd)

To make

Before the beading is worked a gathered ribbon is stitched to the two edges.

1 Prepare ribbon by rolling and overcasting each raw end with gold metallic sewing thread, then run a gathering stitch down one selvage edge of ribbon. Pin middle of ribbon to middle point of pillow edge. Pin one end to left edge and the other to right edge.

2 Pull up gathering thread, urging ribbon into neat gathers as you go. Then pin ribbon to pillow edge every few inches (centimeters), stitch securely using small stitches, and secure thread end neatly. You are now ready to work the beaded trimming.

3 Using pins as markers (fig 2), measure one edge, and at center point E, push in a pin vertically to mark it. Mark left point A and right point I side seams in the same way.

4 At points A, E, and I work a long drop. Thread 1 brz roc, 1 5m amb bd, 1 1cm yel crs, 1 6m amb fc bd, 1 lg gld roc, 10 iri gld roc, 1 org roc, 1 5m brz fc bd, 3 org roc; pass needle up through the 1 5m brz fc bd and 1 org roc; thread 10 iri gld roc and pass needle up through 1st 5 beads threaded, pull thread neatly so that drop hangs straight (fig 1), and make a fastening-off stitch.

5 Measure middle point between center and both sides, and mark again with a pin. Mark also ⅝" (1.5cm) to the right of left side mark, ⅝" (1.5cm) to the left of right side mark and ⅝" (1.5cm) on either side of center point (fig 2).

6 At points B and H work a drop. Thread 1 org roc, 1 5m brz fc bd, 1 iri gld roc, 1 8m amb fc bd, 1 org roc, 1 1cm yel crs, 1 org roc, 1 8m amb fc bd, 1 iri gld roc; pass needle up through the 1 5m brz fc bd and 1 org roc, pull into a circular drop and fasten off (fig 3).

7 Measure center point between C and D, and F and G, and mark with pins.

8 Begin now at point C. Thread 1 lg gld roc, 7 iri gld roc, 1 iri amb roc, 1 5m amb bd, 3 iri amb roc; pass needle up through the 1 5m amb bd and 1 iri amb roc. Thread 7 iri gld roc, 1 lg gld roc and stitch into middle point between C and D. Thread 1 iri amb roc, 1 5m brz fc bd, 1 iri amb roc; pass needle up through 1st 2 beads threaded and stitch again through middle point; repeat previous threading and stitch to point D (fig 4).

9 Repeat another set of beading as shown in fig 4 between points F and G.

10 Repeat instructions to work opposite side of pillow.

fig 1

fig 2

| | 4 (10) | ⅝ (1.5) | 3 (7) | ⅝ (1.5) | ⅝ (1.5) | 3 (7) | ⅝ (1.5) | 4 (10) | in (cm) |

A   B   C   D   E   F   G   H   I

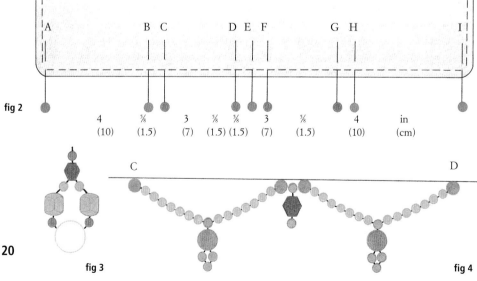

fig 3

fig 4

Yellow brocade pillow

You will need

11" (28cm) square pillow
Polyester thread
Needle fine enough to pass through
    beads twice when threaded
248 large iridescent turquoise rocailles
    (lg iri turq roc)

To make

This pillow is trimmed with the beaded
triangle as seen on page 15, this time
repeated as an edging.

1 Using pins as markers, measure and
mark one edge as shown in fig 1.

126 large gold rocailles (lg gld roc)
104 orange rocailles (org roc)
10 8mm-diam turquoise faceted crystals
    (8m turq fc crs)
8 5mm-diam turquoise crystals
    (5m turq crs)

roc, 1 iri turq roc, 1 iri turq roc, 1 lg gld
roc, 1 lg iri turq roc between each pair
of lg iri turq roc of 1st row. Following
fig 2, continue to work rest of triangle,
finishing with 8m turq fc crs and bead
picot as shown. Work one of these
triangles between points C and D, E and
F, G and H, I and J.

4 Now restart thread at point B, and
measure and mark with pins 7 equal
spaces to point C: each space will
accommodate one bead.

5 Working from point B to point C,
thread 3 org roc and stitch into seam at
2nd pin, in order to form an org roc
picot. Now stitch 1 lg iri turq roc, 1 lg
gld roc, 1 lg iri turq roc between next 3
pins and then pass needle back through
last bead stitched.

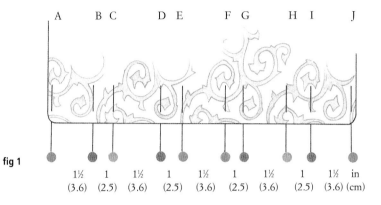

A	B	C	D	E	F	G	H	I	J
1½	1	1½	1	1½	1	1½	1	1½	in
(3.6)	(2.5)	(3.6)	(2.5)	(3.6)	(2.5)	(3.6)	(2.5)	(3.6)	(cm)

fig 1

2 Starting at either left or right side
seam line, begin to work the edging.
The following instructions assume you
are working from left to right.

3 To work 1st triangle, stitch 7 lg iri turq
roc evenly to pillow edge between
points A and B, then pass needle back
through last bead stitched to work 2nd
row. Interlace 1 lg iri turq roc, 1 lg gld

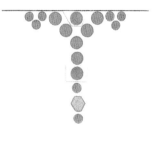

fig 3

6 Interlace 1 lg iri turq roc, then
another, and continue to work beading
following fig 3. When the 5m turq crs
and 1 org bead have been threaded,
pass needle up through the 5m turq crs
and rest of beading to work next 3 org
roc picot.

7 Run thread invisibly through seam line
to point D and work the same sequence
(steps 5 and 6) between points D and E,
F and G, H and I.

8 Repeat all instructions given above to
work beaded edging on opposite side
of pillow.

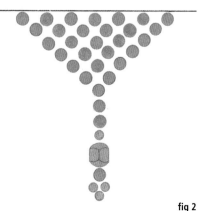

fig 2

21

grapes & vine leaves

The striking vine leaves incorporated into these two chokers are an unusual example of the openwork or beaded lace technique described on page 14. Used here to create an interesting three-dimensional effect, it is combined with two methods of bead threading to create the bunches of bead "grapes." The same methods can also be used to make clusters of beads forming decorative drops to be used as trimming for pillows, tie-backs, or as edgings for garments and soft funishings.

The basic pattern for the two chokers seen here is identical.

You will need

Polyester thread

Needle fine enough to pass through beads and bugles twice when threaded

For crystal choker:

16" (40cm) approx velvet ribbon (or take your neck measurement), ⅝" (1.5cm) wide; add 2" (5cm) for finishing

1½" (4cm) velcro fastening

Vine-leaf beads:

  463 green rocailles (roc)

  101 6mm iridescent green bugles (bg)

  15 4mm iridescent green bugles (sm bg)

Grape beads:

  10 1cm-diam pink faceted crystals

  6 1cm-diam purplish-blue faceted beads

Grape stems:

  38 pink crystal rocailles

  36 purple rocailles

  18 4mm pink bugles

  16 6mm iridescent purple bugles

For garnet choker:

Ribbon and velcro fastening:

  as for crystal choker

Vine-leaf beads: as for crystal choker

Grape beads:

  46 5mm-diam garnet or purple glass beads

Grape stems:

  23 small bronze metallic beads

  15 small amber glass beads

  4 6mm bronze bugles

  2 large amber beads

  1 pinky bronze bead

  1 green-bronze bead

To work vine leaves for both chokers

1 Prepare the thread. Cut a 3¼yd (3m) length and find center point by placing ends together. Make an overhand knot and slip a pin into it before pulling thread tight. Push pin into your cork board to secure the thread.

2 You will work right-hand side of vine leaf first, so thread a needle onto one end of thread and carefully place end without needle to left-hand side of board, while you are working with needle-threaded length.

To work right-hand side

Work from center to right-hand side edge as follows:

1st row (fig 1) Thread 1 bg, 1 roc, 1 bg, 1 roc, 1 bg, 1 roc, 1 bg, 2 roc, 1 bg, 2 roc, 1 bg, 2 roc, 1 bg, 2 roc, 1 bg, 3 roc, 1 bg, 3 roc, 1 bg, 3 roc, 1 bg, 3 roc, 1 sm bg, 4 roc. Now make a picot of last 3 beads by passing needle up through 4th to last bead of this row.

2nd row (fig 2) This row will begin to shape the "lace" structure and it will become progressively easier to work. Thread 1 sm bg, 3 roc; pass needle up through bugle K of 1st row; 3 roc, 1 bg, 3 roc; pass needle up through bugle I of 1st row; 3 roc, 1 bg, 2 roc; pass needle up through bugle G of 1st row, 2 roc, 1 bg, 2 roc; pass needle up through bugle E of 1st row; 2 roc, 1 bg, 1 roc; pass needle up through bugle C of 1st row; 1 roc, 1 bg, 1 roc; pass needle up through bugle A of 1st row.

3rd row (fig 3) Thread 2 roc, 1 bg, 1 roc; pass needle down through bugle B of 2nd row; 1 roc, 1 bg, 1 roc; pass needle down through bugle D of 2nd row; 2 roc, 1 bg, 2 roc; pass needle down through bugle F of 2nd row; 2 roc, 1 bg, 2 roc; pass needle down through bugle H of 2nd row; 3 roc, 1 bg, 3 roc; pass needle down through bugle J of 2nd row; 3 roc, 1 sm bg, 4 roc. Make a picot of last 3 beads by passing needle up through 4th to last bead of this row.

4th row (fig 4) Thread 1 sm bg, 3 roc, 1 bg, 3 roc; pass needle up through bugle I of 3rd row; 3 roc, 1 bg, 2 roc; pass needle up through bugle G of 3rd row; 2 roc, 1 bg, 2 roc; pass needle up through bugle E of 3rd row; 2 roc, 1 bg, 1 roc; pass needle up through bugle C of 3rd row; 1 roc, 1 bg, 1 roc; pass needle up through bugle A of 3rd row.

5th row (fig 5) Thread 3 roc, 1 bg, 1 roc; pass needle down through bugle B of 4th row; 1 roc, 1 bg, 1 roc; pass needle down through bugle D of 4th row; 2

fig 1   fig 2

A   A

B   B

C   C

D   D

E   E

F   F

G   G

H   H

I   I

J   J

K   K

roc, 1 bg, 2 roc; pass needle down through bugle F of 4th row; 2 roc, 1 bg, 2 roc; pass needle down through bugle H of 4th row; 3 roc, 1 bg, 3 roc; pass needle down through bugle J of 4th row.

6th row (fig 6) Thread 5 roc, 1 bg, 3 roc; pass needle up through bugle I of 5th row; 3 roc, 1 bg, 2 roc; pass needle up through bugle G of 5th row; 2 roc, 1 bg, 2 roc; pass needle up through bugle E of 5th row; 2 roc, 1 bg, 1 roc; pass needle up through bugle C of 5th row; 1 roc, 1 bg, 1 roc; pass needle up through bugle A of 5th row.

7th row (fig 7) Thread 5 roc, 1 bg, 1 roc; pass needle down through bugle B of 6th row; 1 roc, 1 bg, 1 roc; pass needle down through bugle D of 6th row; 2 roc, 1 bg, 2 roc; pass needle down through bugle F of 6th row; 2 roc, 1 bg, 2 roc; pass needle down through bugle H of 6th row.

8th row (fig 8) Thread 7 roc, 1 bg, 2 roc; pass needle up through bugle G of 7th row; 2 roc, 1 bg, 2 roc; pass needle up through bugle E of 7th row; 2 roc, 1 bg, 1 roc; pass needle up through bugle C of 7th row; 1 roc, 1 bg, 1 roc; now pass needle up through bugle A of 7th row.

9th row Thread 8 roc, 1 bg, 1 roc; pass needle down through bugle B of 8th row; 1 roc, 1 bg, 1 roc; pass needle down through bugle D of 8th row; 2 roc, 1 bg, 2 roc; pass needle down through bugle F of 8th row; 3 roc, 1 sm bg, 4 roc. Now make a picot of last 3 beads by passing needle up through 4th to last bead of this row.

10th row Thread 1 sm bg, 3 roc, 1 bg, 2 roc; pass needle up through bugle E of 9th row; 2 roc, 1 bg, 1 roc; pass needle up through bugle C of 9th row; 1 roc, 1 bg, 1 roc; pass needle up through bugle A of 9th row.

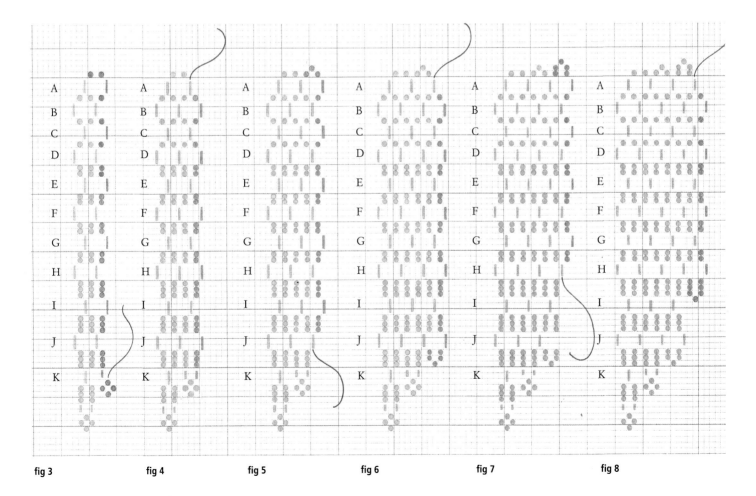

fig 3   fig 4   fig 5   fig 6   fig 7   fig 8

11th row Thread 12 roc, 1 bg, 1 roc; pass needle down through bugle B of 10th row; 1 roc, 1 bg, 1 roc; pass needle down through bugle D of 10th row; 3 roc, 1 sm bg, 4 roc. Now make a picot of last 3 beads by passing needle up through 4th to last bead of this row.

12th row (fig 9) Thread 1 sm bg, 3 roc, 1 bg, 1 roc; pass needle up through bugle C of 11th row; 6 roc, 1 bg, 1 roc; pass needle over thread below bugle A of 11th row to form a loop and return needle through last bead and bugle of 12th row.

13th row Thread 3 roc; pass needle down through 2nd last bead of 12th row and pull tight to make a picot; 1 roc, 1 bg, 4 roc. Now make a picot of last 3 beads by passing needle through 4th to last bead of this row; 1 bg, 1 roc; pass needle down through 5th, 6th, and 7th to last beads of 12th row. Make a

few fastening-off stitches around 12th row thread (fig 10), then pass needle down through rest of 12th row and cut off thread end neatly.

To work left-hand side

1 Remove pin from cork board and undo knot of thread around it. Thread 1¾yd (1.5m) length which was laid to left-hand side of board and pin down middle loop of thread of beading already worked between 1st and 2nd rows, to secure it while you work.

2 Now work from right to left, that is from center to left-hand side edge. Fig 11 shows the complete vine leaf: 1st and 2nd rows of right-hand side instructions you have just worked form the center of the whole structure, so consider right-hand side 1st row as 2nd row for left-hand side, and work 3rd to 13th rows from center out to left-hand edge using same threading instructions.

fig 10

fig 9

fig 11

To work the grapes

fig 12

fig 13

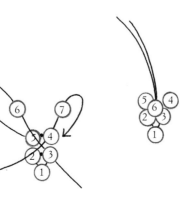

Crystal choker grapes (fig 12) The sequence of working is from bottom grape A up to point N.

1 Cut a 30" (75cm) length of thread and thread a needle on both ends. Find the center of the thread and, with one needle, thread on 1 purple rocaille and push down to this center point. Thread on 1 1cm-diam pink faceted crystal next to this and take 2nd needle through this bead as well.

2 Referring to color threading sequence in fig 12, continue to thread with both needles through same beads to point B after 1st 6mm iridescent purple bugle.

3 Using only one needle and thread, follow sequence to point C and return to point B. Using both needles and threads, thread to point D.

4 Using longest of the 2 threads, work to point F and continue in this way, always using longest of threads when you make a "spur" off to G, K, J, and M, until you reach point N.

5 Work another "stem" of grapes in same way, tying point B between the 2 working threads at point N, giving a cluster effect to this stem.

Garnet choker grapes

1 Cut two 1¼yd (1m) lengths of thread and thread a needle onto each of the 4 ends.

2 Referring to fig 14, using one length of thread with 2 needles per branch, work 2 separate branches: one with a 9- and 17-grape bunch, and the other with a 7- and 13-grape bunch, following the steps shown in fig 13. The sequence of

fig 14

working is from A and B upward to point C in fig 14.

3 Join the 2 branches at point C (fig 14) by threading all 4 ends through the 6mm bronze bugles and the 4 larger beads in sequence – 2 amber, 1 pinky bronze, and 1 green-bronze – to blend end of grape stem in with vine leaf.

To attach grape bunches to vine leaves
Tie and knot the relevant bunches around vine-leaf thread at base of bugle A in fig 1, on page 24. Thread remaining ends individually through some of the beads and bugles of the vine-leaf structure and then cut them off neatly.

To attach beading to velvet band
Sew choker beading to velvet band by catching with small stitches below each bugle bead in row A.

Turn under ends of velvet ribbon and stitch on velcro fastening neatly to cover the raw ends.

Beading in the round

Having explored the technique of beading in rows, you can move on to beading in rounds to create a circular effect. It is also easy to do, and again involves no more than a needle and thread.

Circular beading can be worked flat – to create a lace doily, for example. By consistently using the same number of beads in each row you can make a tubular shape, as illustrated by the circular-beaded bracelet on the next page. Finally, by increasing or decreasing the number of beads per round you can shape the beading to decorate shaped items, such as the perfume bottles in this chapter.

circular beading

Circular beading can be used to work some simple but very effective projects, from chokers and straps to belts and bracelets. By working in rounds rather than in rows you can create three-dimensional, tubular shapes. You can increase the length of the beading by measuring the number of rounds to an inch (or a centimeter) and increasing the total number of rounds accordingly. Alternatively, by using the technique of beadwrapping you can make lengths of beaded cord that will be stronger and harder-wearing.

Starting off

1 Thread a number of beads onto your working thread. Tie thread together to form a continuous circle of beads: this gives you the base or 1st round. Pass needle again through 1st bead threaded to begin working 2nd round (fig 1).

2 Work the 2nd round of beads, suspending a bead for 2nd round between a pair of beads of 1st round (fig 2).

3 Begin to work the 3rd round, taking needle and thread from the last bead threaded for 2nd round and passing it again through 1st bead threaded for 2nd round (fig 3).

4 Continue in this way (fig 4), pulling thread tight at end of each round, and work about 100 rounds, depending on length needed.

NB The bracelet seen in the photograph took 111 rounds.

fig 1	fig 2	fig 3	fig 4

The beading will start to form a tube after 4 or 5 rounds, and should be easy to work holding the tube between the fingers of your non-threading hand. You can slip the tube as it forms onto a pen, pencil, or chopstick, depending on the diameter of the project, to use as a core to support the beading. This support can be slipped out later. With practice you should find this support unnecessary.

Finishing off

fig 5

You can create a simple fastening for a bracelet or a necklace by following the steps outlined below. Alternatively, decorate the end of the loop with a bead drop and picot. You can make an adjustable fastening by using a short string of beads with a drop in the middle and at the end. Choose between these drops, depending on the size of your wrist.

1 Make a fastening-off stitch to form a cross between the circle of threaded beads in last round (fig 5). Attach a large bead and a small bead. Take needle back through large bead and make a fastening-off stitch. Stitch thread through beads of last few rounds. Make 2 or 3 fastening-off stitches and cut off thread neatly.

2 Put thread of other end into a needle and thread on sufficient large rocailles to make a loop which will slip over large beads of other end, then pass needle through 1st bead threaded to complete the loop.

3 Make 2 or 3 fastening-off stitches and thread through beads of last round. Cut off thread neatly.

Beadwrapping

Using the technique of beadwrapping, where beads threaded onto a continuous thread are wrapped and wound around a prepared cord core, it is possible to make lengths of beaded cord. These can be worked quite quickly to make chokers, bracelets, belts, bell pulls, and many other items. So far, the techniques described have usually required careful planning and charting of beads and colors, but beadwrapping is worked to best effect with beads of one size, the chosen colors being threaded onto the working thread more or less randomly.

Making a cord core

You will need
Length of 3-strand cord
Polyester thread, color matched
   to cord

Needle fine enough to pass through
   beads twice when threaded
Selection of similar-sized beads

To make the core
1 Carefully whip ends of cord to prevent it unraveling, by wrapping thread around ends at least 6 times (fig 1). Fasten off and cut off any excess thread.
2 Lay cord on a flat surface in a closed circle with the 2 ends butted together (fig 2).
3 Stitch these ends to the cord they are

lying against, being careful not to pull too tightly. Then stitch a few times between whipping of each end. This will form a "bridge" and make the cord circle continuous (fig 3).
NB If using the cord core for upholstery tie-backs, set the join off-center so that when the cords are knotted together they have maximum flexibility.

fig 1

fig 2

fig 3

Wrapping the beads

1 Starting at one end of cord core, fasten on the working thread 1" (2.5cm) from end. This will form a loop from which to make a fastening for a belt, choker, or bracelet, or a loop from which to hang a tie-back or a bell pull. You can vary the size of the loops depending on the fastening you are using. Thread on about 24 beads in a sequence of your choice.
2 Holding thread taut with beads pushed together, wind beaded length

around cord core, pulling tightly. Holding wrapped beading firmly, stitch a few times through unwrapped cord next to beads, then pass needle through last 2 or 3 beads threaded (see position of needle in photograph).
3 Continue to thread, wind, and stitch until you reach 1" (2.5cm) from other end, and fasten off neatly.
NB For ease of working, do not try to wrap too many rounds of beads before stitching through the cord.

Finishing off

1 Use a glass button with a shank and place the shank between one of the cord loops.
2 Secure by stitching through the cord, together with the shank, and the other side of the cord loop.
3 Loop the other loop over this to make the fastening.

For a stylish finishing touch, try using a beautiful button in combination with simple beading. The fastening will then become the prominent feature of the design. You can be as inventive as you like, and experiment with decorative tassel fastenings or a beaded loop fastening, as appropriate.

perfume bottles

As in the Grapes and Vine Leaves bead lace chokers on page 22, by varying the threading sequence and number of beads you can create an openwork effect, but this time you will be working in rounds instead of rows. Depending on the shape chosen, by increasing or decreasing the number of beads per round it is possible to decorate shaped objects with beading, and this is the technique used for the perfume bottles here.

Adorned with openwork beading, one of these perfume bottles is finished with a final round of elegant teardrops, the other with beautiful crystal drops.

Teardrop perfume bottle

You will need

4¼yd (4m) polyester thread
Needle fine enough to pass through
   smallest bead twice when threaded
150 pearly blue rocailles (pbl roc)
140 sea-green rocailles (s-gr roc)
90 small yellow cut bd (sm yel cut bd)
40 large gold rocailles (lg gld roc)
40 6mm blue bugles (6m bl bg)
40 iridescent green rocailles (iri gr roc)
32 large turquoise rocailles (lg turq roc)
30 large dark blue rocailles (lg dk bl roc)
30 turquoise rocailles (turq roc)
30 small dark blue crystals (sm dk bl crs)

20 dark green rocailles (dk gr roc)
20 green rocailles (gr roc)
20 pale blue glass teardrops (ple bl tdp)
20 4mm turquoise bugles (4m turq bg)
20 small blue pearls (sm bl pl)
20 small pale blue crystals (sm ple bl crs)
10 medium blue-gray pearls
   (med bl-g pl)
10 large pale turquoise crystals
   (lg ple turq crs)
10 large pale green crystals
   (lg ple gr crs)
1 blue flat crystal (bl flt crs)
1 small pale green crystal (sm ple gr crs)

To make

The beading is worked down from the
bottle neck. The illustration (fig 1) shows
the openwork effect you are creating.

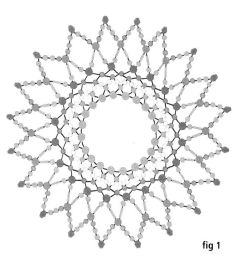

fig 1

1st round Thread 20 lg turq roc, then tie
these around bottle neck and knot
thread so that you have a 1¼yd (1m)
end and a 3¼yd (3m) end of thread. To
prevent tangles, wind up shorter length
and tuck it into bottle ready for use
later. Now continue with longer length
threaded into needle.

2nd round Thread 1 s-gr roc between
each pair of lg turq roc of 1st round,
then pass needle again through 1st
bead of this round.

3rd round Thread 1 sm yel cut bd, 1 s-gr
roc, 1 sm yel cut bd as a picot between
each pair of s-gr roc of 2nd round, then

pass needle again through 1st and 2nd
bead of 1st picot (fig 2).

4th round Thread 1 pbl roc between

fig 2

each pair of s-gr roc of 3rd round, then
pass needle again through 1st pbl roc of
this round.

5th round Thread 1 lg dk bl roc between
each pair of pbl roc of 4th round, then
pass needle again through 1st lg dk bl
roc of this round.

6th round Thread 1 sm b pl, 1 4m turq
bg, 1 lg gld roc, 1 4m turq bg, 1 sm bl
pl into every other lg dk bl roc of 5th
round. This will make 10 loops of beads.
Then pass needle again through 1st 3
beads of 1st loop in this round (fig 3).

7th round Thread 1 pbl roc, 2 iri gr roc,
1 sm dk bl crs, 2 iri gr roc, 1 pbl roc into

fig 3

every lg gld roc of 6th round, then pass
needle again through 1st 4 beads of
this round (fig 4).

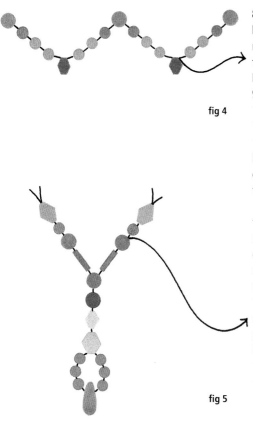

fig 4

fig 5

8th round Thread 1 dk gr roc, 1 6m bl bg, 1 lg ple turq crs, 1 6m bl bg, 1 dk gr roc into every sm dk bl crs of 7th round, then pass needle again through 1st 3 beads of this round.

9th round Thread 1 pbl roc, 1 lg gld roc, 1 6m bl bg, 1 lg turq roc, 1 lg dk bl roc, 1 sm ple bl crs, 1 lg ple gr crs, 3 s-gr roc, 1 ple bl tdp, 3 s-gr roc, then pass needle back through the lg ple gr crs, sm ple bl crs, lg dk bl roc, lg turq roc, and pull up to form a drop. Then thread 1 6m bl bg, 1 lg gld roc, 1 pbl roc, and pass needle through lg ple turq crs of 8th round. Repeat this sequence between each pair of lg ple turq crs of 8th round, then pass needle again through 1st 2 beads of this round (fig 5).

10th round Thread 2 s-gr roc, 1 lg gld roc, 1 sm dk bl crs, 1 ple bl tdp, then pass needle back up through the sm dk bl crs and lg gld roc. Then thread 2 s-gr roc, and pass needle through next lg gld roc of 9th round. Repeat this sequence between each pair of lg gld roc of 9th round (fig 6).

Finish by making fastening-off stitches around working thread between beads, and passing needle through several beads before cutting off remaining thread neatly.

To work bottle neck

Rethread needle with the 1¼yd (1m) length of thread which was tucked into bottle neck and work bottle neck up:

fig 6

1st round Thread 1 sm yel cut bd, 1 sm dk bl crs, 1 sm yel cut bd between every lg turq roc of bottle 1st round, then pass needle again through 1st 2 beads of this round.

2nd round Thread 1 sm ple bl crs between each pair of sm dk bl crs of 1st round, then pass needle again through 1st sm ple bl crs of this round.

3rd round Thread 1 med bl-g pl between each pair of sm ple bl crs of 2nd round, then pass needle again through 1st med bl-g pl of this round.

4th round Thread 1 s-gr roc, 1 sm yel cut bd between each pair of med bl-g pl of 3rd round, then pass needle again through 1st 2 beads of this round.

5th round Thread 1 sm dk bl crs between each pair of sm yel cut bd of 4th round, then pass needle again through 1st bead of this round.

6th round Thread 3 pbl roc between each pair of sm dk bl crs of 5th round, then pass needle again through 1st 2 beads of this round.

7th round Thread 1 pbl roc, 1 lg turq roc, 1 pbl roc between pairs of the middle 3 pbl roc of 6th round, then pass needle again through 1st 2 beads of this round.

8th round Thread 1 sm yel cut bd, 1 sm dk bl crs, 1 sm yel cut bd between each pair of lg turq roc of 7th round, then pass needle again through 1st 2 beads of this round.

9th round Thread 1 turq roc, 1 pbl roc, 1 turq roc between each pair of sm dk bl crs of 8th round, then pull up thread tightly. Finish by making fastening-off stitches around working thread between beads, and passing needle through several beads before cutting off thread.

To work bottle stopper drop

Thread 1 lg turq roc, 1 sm ple gr crs, 1 bl flt crs, 1 lg dk bl crs, 1 turq roc, then pass needle back up through 1st 4 beads to make a drop. Tie this tightly around ring of stopper and pass threads back down through the beads, before cutting off remaining thread neatly.

Crystal drop perfume bottle

You will need

4¼yd (4m) polyester thread
Needle fine enough to pass through
   smallest bead twice when threaded
145 jade rocailles (jd roc)
136 large turquoise rocailles
   (lg turq roc)
99 Delft blue rocailles (Dbl roc)
90 dark green rocailles (dk gr roc)

84 blue flat crystals (bl flt crs)
45 large dark blue rocailles (lg dk bl roc)
37 small sea-green cut beads
   (sm s-gr cut bd)
37 small dark blue crystals
   (sm dk bl crs)
18 silver metallic beads (silv met bd)
10 large blue crystals (lg bl crs)
9 large turquoise crystals (lg turq crs)

To make

The beading is worked down from the
bottle neck.

1st round Thread 18 lg dk bl roc, then
tie these around bottle neck and knot
thread so that you have a 1¼yd (1m)
end and a 3¼yd (3m) end of thread. To
prevent tangles, wind up shorter length
and tuck it into bottle for use later.
Now continue with longer length
threaded into needle.

2nd round Thread 1 jd roc between each
pair of lg dk bl roc in 1st round, then
pass needle again through 1st bead of
this round.

3rd round Thread 1 lg turq roc between
each pair of jd roc in 2nd round, then
pass needle again through 1st bead of
this round.

4th round Thread 1 dk gr roc, 1 Dbl roc,
1 dk gr roc between each pair of lg turq
roc in 3rd round, then pass needle again
through 1st bead of this round.

5th round Thread 3 jd roc, 1 sm s-gr cut
bd, 1 lg dk bl roc, 1 sm s-gr cut bd, 3 jd
roc into every other Dbl roc of 4th

1 dk gr roc, 3 lg turq roc into every lg dk
bl roc of 5th round, then pass needle
again through 1st 6 beads of this round.

7th round Thread 1 sm s-gr cut bd, 3 jd
roc, 1 lg dk bl roc, 1 lg bl crs, 1 lg dk bl
roc, 3 jd roc, 1 sm s-gr cut bd into every
sm dk bl crs of 6th round. Pass needle
again through 1st 6 beads of this round.

8th round Thread 1 dk gr roc, 1 lg turq
roc, 2 Dbl roc, 1 lg turq crs, 2 Dbl roc, 1
lg turq roc, 1 dk gr roc into every lg bl
crs of 7th round, then pass needle again
through 1st 6 beads of this round
(fig 2).

9th round Thread 1 dk gr roc, 1 lg dk bl
roc, 1 jd roc, 1 Dbl roc, 1 jd roc, 1 lg dk
bl roc, 1 dk gr roc into every middle Dbl
roc, lg turq crs, Dbl roc of 8th round
(fig 3).

10th round Thread 1 sm dk bl crs, 3 bl flt
crs, 1 lg turq roc, then pass needle up
through 3 bl flt crs, 1 sm dk bl crs to
form a "drop." Work a drop each side
of the lg turq crs of 8th round and each
side of the Dbl roc of 9th round,
forming 27 drops in total (fig 4). Finish

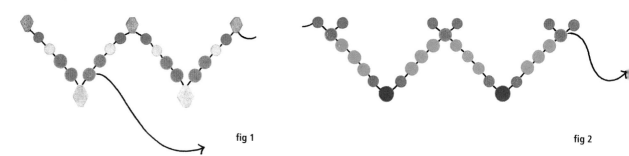

fig 1

fig 2

round, then pass needle again through
1st 5 beads of this round (fig 1).
6th round Thread 3 lg turq roc, 1 dk gr
roc, 1 Dbl roc, 1 sm dk bl crs, 1 Dbl roc,

off by making fastening-off stitches
around remaining thread and passing
needle through several beads before
cutting off remaining thread neatly.

fig 3

fig 4

To work bottle neck

Rethread needle with the ⅛yd (1m) length of thread which was tucked into bottle neck and work bottle neck upward, as follows:

1st round Thread 1 lg turq roc between each pair of lg dk bl roc of 1st round of bottle beading.

2nd round Thread 1 silv met bd between each pair of lg turq roc of 1st round. Finish off thread neatly as before.

To work bottle stopper drop

Thread 1 sm s-gr cut bd, 1 lg bl crs, 1 jd roc, 1 sm dk bl crs, 3 bl flt crs, 1 lg turq roc, then pass needle back up through 1st 7 beads to make a drop. Tie this tightly around ring of stopper and pass threads back down through the beads, before cutting off thread neatly.

Bottle stopper variation

You could make a small tassel drop as follows:

1 Using approximately 16" (40cm) of polyester thread, tie one end around stopper ring, leaving an 3¼" (8cm) "tail," and thread other end into a needle. Thread on 1 large rocaille, 1 large faceted bead, 1 large rocaille.

2 Thread on 11 rocailles and pass needle up through 1st 10 rocailles threaded and large rocaille, large faceted bead, and 1st large rocaille threaded.

3 Pass needle over stopper ring and down through 1st 3 beads threaded. Thread on 11 rocailles and pass needle up through 1st 10 rocailles threaded and 1st 3 beads threaded.

4 Repeat step 3 four times more, so that tassel has 6 beaded strands.

5 Pass needle again over stopper ring, and make 3 or 4 fastening-off stitches around group of threads between stopper ring and 1st large rocaille.

6 Pass needle down through 1st 3 beads threaded and cut thread off neatly.

7 Thread tail into needle and pass down through 1st 3 beads threaded and cut off neatly.

beadwrapped tie-back

Here two lengths of beadwrapping are knotted together to create an unusual, chunky, textural effect. This attractive tie-back is worked with beads of one size, threaded onto the working thread more or less at random. You could experiment with different color themes by deciding on a dominant color and threading more beads of that color, along with occasional beads of the less dominant or highlight color, or you could try using beads of different sizes. Bear in mind that, in the latter case, more of the cord will show but you could use this to your advantage, making the cord a part of the design.

You can change the dimensions of the tie-back by following the calculations given here. For more information about the technique of beadwrapping see page 31.

fig 1

You will need

For a tie-back 12" (30cm) approx in length:
76" (193cm) beige 3-strand cord, ¼" (5mm) in diameter
7¾yd (7m) beige polyester thread
Needle fine enough to pass through beads twice when threaded
1300 large violet rocailles (lg vio roc)
1300 large champagne rocailles (lg chm roc)
1300 large iridescent amber rocailles (lg iri amb roc)

To make cord core

1 Cut the cord in half and then carefully whip the 4 ends by wrapping thread around ends at least 6 times. Fasten off any excess thread and cut off neatly.
2 Follow the instructions on page 31 to make 2 identical cords.

To wrap the beads

1 Starting at end of cord core, fasten on working thread 2.5cm (1in) from end. This will form a loop from which to hang the tie-back. Thread about 24 rocailles in your chosen sequence, for example: 2 lg chm roc, 3 lg vio roc, 1 lg chm roc, 2 lg iri amb roc, 2 lg chm roc, 2 lg vio roc, 3 lg chm roc, 3 lg iri amb roc, 1 lg chm roc, 3 lg vio roc, 2 lg chm roc, etc.
2 Holding thread taut and with beads pushed together side by side, wind beaded length around cord core, pull tightly. Holding wrapped beading firmly, stitch a few times through unwrapped cord next to beads, then pass needle through last 2 or 3 beads threaded.
3 Continue to thread, wind and stitch, until you reach 1" (2.5cm) from other end of cord core, and fasten off neatly.
4 Repeat all above instructions with other length of cord core to make second tie-back.

The knot

1 Lay one length of beadwrapping on a flat surface to form a crossed loop.
2 Interlace other length with it, being careful to keep loops even. This forms a knot known as the Carrick Bend or Josephine Knot (fig 1).

To alter tie-back dimensions

If longer tie-backs are required, for instance for use with heavy velvet draperies, decide on the length and use the following formula for estimating the length of thread and number of beads required for a core made from cord ¼" (5mm) diameter.

To calculate length of thread

Allow 1½" (4cm) polyester thread for each "wrap" around the cord
Allow 9 wraps per inch (3 wraps per cm)
Length of thread required per inch (cm) of cord = 9 x 1½ (4 x 3) = 13½" (12cm)
Total length of thread required = 13½ (12) x length of cord in inches (cm)

To calculate number of beads

Allow 12 beads approx per wrap, using large rocailles
Allow 9 wraps per inch (3 wraps per cm)
Number of beads required per cm (inch) of cord = 9 x 12 (3 x 12) = 108 (36)
Total number of beads required = 108 (36) x length of cord in inches (cm)

Beaded finishes

The jewel-like quality of light reflected by beaded buttons and tassels gives an extra dimension to even simple objects. We have already seen beads used as a trimming on pillows, using simple needlewoven beading. This chapter contains more ideas for decorative bead finishes, from a beautiful button gracing the end of a bolster and a glorious beaded trim on a pretty drawstring bag, to glittering tassels imparting style and glamour to a velvet scarf. Finishing touches such as these are not complicated, involving no more than threading a needle and a little stitching.

buttons & tassels

Handmade beaded buttons are not difficult to make and lend style to soft furnishings and a touch of originality to fashion accessories. You can either make your own buttons or decorate ready-made fabric ones. Instead of using beads you can also use sequins (for sequin button design ideas see page 104).

Decorative beaded tassels are another attractive beaded finish and make a striking addition to many accessories. To create your own tassel designs, see also page 104.

One simple way of making a beaded button is to wrap small beads over a large bead. This is the method used to make the cufflinks (see below) but you could also use it for a tassel head or to create an original finish for a cushion.

1 Using a strong polyester thread matched to beads, thread a short length through the large bead hole, pass it over outside curve of bead and back to hole

fig 1   fig 2   fig 3   fig 4   fig 5

fig 6

first entered, tie ends together and knot (fig 1). Pull this loop of thread to push knot inside bead hole shaft (fig 2).
2 Thread long end of thread into a needle and pass it into the large bead hole, stitching through thread loop at top hole edge (fig 3). Thread on as

many small beads as will cover curve of large bead from top to bottom hole, say 9. Pass needle under thread loop (fig 4). Fasten off, then pass needle down through last bead threaded.
3 Thread on 2 less beads than before (7), pass over curve of large bead and through 1st bead threaded (fig 5), under thread loop, and then make a fastening-off stitch. Repeat this, alternating 9, 7, 9, 7 beads, until large bead is covered with small beads. The thread will have formed a buttonhole-type stitch around top and bottom holes (fig 6). The alternating numbers of beads will create a smooth profile.
4 Thread a bead onto working end to cover hole neatly, stitch needle through to other hole and knot short and working thread ends together. Trim off short end. Use other to attach button.

Button cufflinks

Wrapped bead buttons can be used to make cufflinks, by joining two together with a link of beads. You can use beads which are the same size or different: in the latter case the larger button becomes the main decorative feature.

1 Make 2 buttons without the centre bead finish. Trim off short ends of threads and thread long end of one through 8 or 9 small beads. Tie this end tightly to end of thread on other button, and knot (fig 7).
2 Pass this end of thread through link of beads, so that there is an end traveling in each direction, and again tie it around other thread, by fastening-off.

3 Take end through hole (fig 8) and thread on a flat crystal and a bead, or a cup sequin (convex side uppermost) and a bead, or a bead large enough to conceal hole, then pass thread through beads to centre of bead link (fig 9).
4 Repeat with other end of thread, and tie ends together at centre of link. Thread each end in opposite directions through link (fig 10). Cut off thread.

fig 7   fig 8   fig 9   fig 10

Beaded flat buttons

To make these, you will need to use fabric-covered buttons. These can either be ready made, or you can make your own using a button-covering kit, making sure that you follow the instructions regarding the grain of the fabric carefully. When deciding what size of button to use, remember to allow for the beads or sequins that will be stitched onto it. It is possible to bead or sequin the fabric before covering the button, but although it may be a little easier to stitch this way, it can be quite tricky to keep the grain of the fabric square and avoid distorting the beading while making the button. For ideas for sequined button designs see page 104.

1 Draw a circle on paper to same diameter as button. Starting at outside edge, lay beads side by side, with hole shafts following line of circle and leaving a small gap between them to accommodate the stitching, until there is a complete circle of beads. This is to calculate how many beads you need.

2 Using a strong polyester thread and the fabric-covered button, make a concealed fastening-on stitch (see page 15) and bring needle out half a bead width from outer edge. Make another fastening-on stitch, thread on a bead and, laying it down, pick up a little of the fabric with the needle to stitch down the bead. Do this with the other beads, spacing them carefully so that they form a continuous circle. If it is possible, draw a circle onto the fabric to follow.

3 Work out how many beads will be needed to make another circle inside outer one, and stitch as before. Repeat with more circles of decreasing diameter, until there is room to stitch only 3 beads or 1 bead in the center. Make a fastening-off stitch, pass needle into fabric, bring it out again, and cut off thread neatly.

Beaded tassels

By varying the number and sequence of beads, and using different strand lengths, you will be able to create a huge range of beautiful beaded tassels, such as those incorporated in the projects on pages 44–51. The individual strands might be designed differently, but they are usually assembled in the same way to form the finished tassel.

Make 2 strands of the tassel by threading them together as 1 string of beads, which will be tied at the center and bent over to form the 2 strands.

1 Decide on length of strands required; then, using a strong polyester thread (or buttonhole thread if using very heavy beads) in the same color as the beads, thread the number of beads which will equal 2 strand lengths.

2 Pinning down one end, or tying thread over last bead threaded to ensure beads do not run off thread, pass other end back through 2nd, 3rd, 4th, 5th, and 6th bead at least, before making a fastening-off stitch over strand thread between 6th and 7th bead. Pass thread up through 7th and 8th bead and again fasten off. Repeat this fastening-off again if beads are heavy, pulling stitches tightly. Now pass thread through next few beads and cut off neatly. Repeat with other end of string of beads.

3 Make 5 or 6 identical strings, depending on thickness of tassel required. Lay strings side by side, and find center point either by measuring or by bending strings in half. Double over another piece of thread and pass both ends through center loop to form a large slip loop. Lay bunch of strings carefully into loop, until loop is at their center points (fig 1). Then tighten loop, creating 10 or 12 strands, depending on the number of strings used.

4 To make a tassel head, slip ends of loop into a larger bead or into a wrapped bead button as described on the opposite page (fig 2).

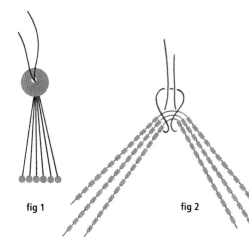

fig 1 fig 2

beaded bolsters

Large buttons decorated with stitched beads, and with beaded tassels and drops, can be used to enhance an interior design scheme. Selecting the color of the beads to accentuate or complement other aspects of the decor can help to coordinate a color scheme, add a touch of richness to enliven an otherwise bland or neutral palette, or intensify an already extravagant one. These bolsters illustrate the versatility of combining beaded accessories.

Purple damask button

You will need

Purple damask-covered button,
    2" (5cm) diameter
Purple polyester thread
Needle fine enough to pass through
    beads twice when threaded
45 large royal-blue rocailles
45 large cherry-red rocailles

To make

1 Divide circumference of button into 10 equal sections, either by marking lightly with tailor's chalk or by using pins as markers (fig 1).

2 Thread 9 large royal-blue rocailles and tie them into a circle, leaving a long and short end of thread. Knot these ends to form a not-too-tight circle of beads. Thread short end through circle of beads and cut off neatly.

3 Using long end, stitch into center point (fig 1, point A) of one of the sections at outer edge, then pass needle in under fabric toward center of button, coming out after about ⅜" (1cm) (point B), and catch down circle of beads by stitching over thread between two beads. Pass needle under fabric to point C and repeat, then pass under fabric to point D and repeat. Fasten off carefully, pass thread into some of the fabric and cut off neatly.

4 Repeat this sequence with a circle of 9 large royal-blue rocailles in every alternate section, and then with a circle of 9 large cherry-red rocailles in remaining sections.

fig 1

Soft crimson button

You will need

Soft crimson needlecord-covered
  button, 1½" (4cm) diameter
Ruby glass embroidery stone, with
  metal claw mount

Crimson polyester thread
Needle fine enough to pass through
  beads twice when threaded
85 large amethyst rocailles (roc)

To make

1 Make a concealed fastening-on stitch
and bring needle out at button center.
Stitch several times through mount.
2 Mark 5 equal sections around base of
stone and, using same length of thread,
thread on 17 roc. Pass needle through
1st 8 roc threaded, and laying circle of
beads down toward outer edge, stitch
over thread on each side of 9th/middle
bead. Pass needle under fabric ¼"
(5mm) to left side and stitch over thread

between top and bottom groups of 4
beads (fig 1). Pass needle under fabric
to right side and repeat. Pass needle
under fabric to base of stone at next pin
marker and repeat. Make 5 petal loops.

fig 1

Pale amethyst crystal loop-tassel button

You will need

Soft crimson needlecord-covered
  button, 1½" (4cm) diameter
Wooden or cut cardboard washer
  shape, 1¼" (3cm) diameter
Maroon, navy, green embroidery thread
8" (20cm) maroon, navy, and green
  3-cord interlaced braid
Pale amethyst sewing thread

Polyester thread
Large-eyed sewing needle; milliner's
  needle
Fabric glue
3,000 2mm pale amethyst cut bugles
  (cut bg)
11 large gold rocailles (roc)
2 gold Chinese-lantern-shaped beads
  with large hole (Ch-ltn bd)

To make

1 Wrap washer with embroidery thread
and glue to button as described for the
bronze tassel-drop button opposite,
using green as main color and navy and
maroon to mark the 6 sections.
2 Bend and stitch 3-cord braid into a
circle. Glue to outside edge of back
of washer.
3 Make 30 strings of 100 cut bg, and

fold them all in half together to make a
loop tassel. Tie thread around ends to
secure. Thread all ends through the 2
Ch-ltn bd, then divide into 6 equal
groups and, using large-eyed needle,
stitch the groups securely into inner
edge of inner hole and back of washer.
4 To finish, tie a circle of 11 roc around
point between the 2 Ch-ltn bds, thread
ends through bead circle. Cut off neatly.

Violet and cherry button

You will need

Violet needlecord-covered button,
  1¾" (4.5cm) diameter
Violet polyester thread

Needle fine enough to pass through
  beads twice when threaded
140 (approx) large cherry-red rocailles

To make

1 Make a concealed fastening-on stitch
and bring out needle at outer edge. Pick
up a cherry-red rocaille, and making a
small stitch, pass needle back under
fabric emerging a bead width away.

2 Continue stitching on rocailles at
random, leaving enough space to allow
fabric to show through.
3 Stitch beads evenly over outer rim of
button, so that there is a regular profile
of beads.

Bronze tassel-drop button

You will need

Purple damask-covered button, 2" (5cm) diameter

Wooden or cut cardboard washer shape, 1¼" (3cm) diameter

Needle fine enough to pass through beads twice when threaded

Gold, pink, and green embroidery thread

Fabric glue

Bronze polyester thread

277 large bronze rocailles (lg brz roc)

16 1cm-diam terracotta 8-grooved round beads (1cm terr 8-g bd)

10 terracotta 4-segmented pear-shaped drop beads (terr 4-seg drp bd)

2 terracotta Chinese-lantern-shaped beads (terr Ch-ltn bd)

To make

1 Wrap gold embroidery thread around washer shape to cover it completely. Mark 6 equal sections with pins, and decorate by wrapping 5 wraps of pink and 5 wraps of green embroidery thread alternately at each section mark.

2 Glue completed washer centrally onto button using strong fabric glue. When completely dry, divide edge of washer into 10 sections, using pins as markers.

3 Make a concealed fastening-on stitch at a pin marker at edge of washer. Thread 5 lg brz roc, 1 1cm terr 8-g bd, 5 lg brz roc, then fasten thread at next pin marker to form a loop of threaded beads. Repeat at each pin marker to form 10 beaded loops around edge of washer. Fasten off securely.

4 Make 10 drops as follows:

1st drop Using bronze polyester thread and leaving a 8" (20cm) tail, thread 40 lg brz roc, 1 terr 4-seg drp bd, 1 lg brz roc; then pass needle up through the terr 4-seg drp bd and 40 lg brz roc, and cut off thread 8" (20cm) beyond last lg brz roc threaded. There will now be two 8" (20cm) lengths of thread to be used for stitching drop to inner edge of washer later (fig 1).

fig 1

Repeat general instructions for making 1st drop, but follow individual threading sequences below for each drop.

2nd drop Thread 15 lg brz roc, 1 1cm terr 8-g bd, 1 lg brz roc, 1 terr Ch-ltn bd, 1 1cm terr 8-g bd, 1 lg brz roc, 1 terr 4-seg drp bd, 1 lg brz roc; pass needle up through all beads threaded after last lg brz roc.

3rd drop Thread 23 lg brz roc, 1 1cm terr 8-g bd, 1 lg brz roc, 1 terr 4-seg drp bd, 1 lg brz roc; pass needle up through all beads threaded after last lg brz roc.

4th drop Thread 5 lg brz roc, 1 1cm terr 8-g bd, 9 lg brz roc, 1 Ch-ltn bd, 5 lg brz roc, 1 terr 4-seg drp bd, 1 lg brz roc; pass needle up through all beads threaded after last lg brz roc.

5th drop Thread 21 lg brz roc, 1 terr 4-seg drp bd, 1 lg brz roc; pass needle up through all beads threaded after last lg brz roc.

6th drop Thread 12 lg brz roc, 1 1cm terr 8-g bd, 1 terr 4-seg drp bd, 1 lg brz roc; pass needle up through all beads threaded after last lg brz roc.

7th drop Thread 10 lg brz roc, 1 terr 4-seg drp bd, 1 lg brz roc; pass needle up through all beads threaded after last lg brz roc.

8th & 9th drop Thread 11 lg brz roc, 1 terr 4-seg drp bd, 1 lg brz roc; pass needle up through all beads threaded after last lg brz roc.

10th drop Thread 5 lg brz roc, 1 1cm terr 8-g bd, 1 terr 4-seg drp bd, 1 lg brz roc; pass needle up through all beads threaded after last lg brz roc.

5 To finish, stitch each drop into inner edge of washer, following figs 2 to 4, taking care to space drops evenly.

fig 2

fig 3

fig 4

47

evening scarf & bag

This elegant velvet scarf is finished at both ends with tassels of colorful crystals, while the bag is trimmed with a lovely netted effect.

Evening scarf

You will need

1¼yd (1m) velvet, 21" (52cm) wide
3¾yd (3.5m) polyester thread
Needle fine enough to pass through
  beads twice when threaded
360 small pale turquoise cut beads
  (sm ple turq cut bd)
260 4mm crystal bugles (4m crs bg)
240 3mm eau-de-nil bugles (3m edn bg)
160 rainbow crystals (rbw crs)
128 silver metallic rocailles (silv met roc)
20 4mm pale turquoise crystals
  (4m ple turq crs)
4 6mm turquoise crystals (6m turq crs)
2 rainbow 8-sided crystals (rbw 8sd crs)

To make

1 With right sides together, fold velvet in half lengthwise. Pin, baste, and stitch down long edge to turn into tube.
2 Turn right side out, and hand stitch one end closed using close gathering stitches. Pull stitches tightly together, at the same time turning under raw edge to conceal it inside tube. Secure with a few stitches across the circular finish (fig 1). Repeat with other end of tube.

To work the tassels

1 Thread 1 silv met roc, 1 4m ple turq crs, 5 silv met roc, 12 3m edn bg, 18 sm ple turq cut bd, 13 4m crs bg, 16 rbw crs, 13 4m crs bg, 18 sm ple turq cut bd, 12 3m edn bg, 5 silv met roc, 1 4m ple turq crs, 1 silv met roc. Fasten off at each end.
2 Work 9 more of these strings and separate them into 2 bunches of 5.
3 Lay down a bunch of 5 strings and follow instructions on page 43 (fig 11).
4 Thread 2 ends of noose thread through 1 silv met roc, 1 6m turq crs, 1 silv met roc, 1 rbw 8sd crs, 1 silv met roc, 1 6m turq crs 1 silv met roc. Attach to center of circular finish. Repeat with other end.

fig 1

Evening bag

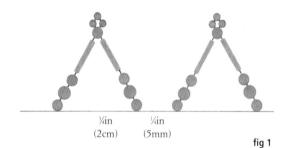

¼in (2cm)   ¼in (5mm)

fig 1

fig 2

You will need

Velvet drawstring bag, 25½" (65cm) in circumference

5½yd (5m) approx polyester thread

5½yd (5m) approx crochet thread

Needle fine enough to pass through smallest bead twice when threaded

600 2mm green-bronze cut bugles (2m gr-brz cut bg)

537 green-bronze cut beads (gr-brz cut bd)

267 6mm iridescent green-gold bugles (6m iri gr-gld bg)

220 large bronze-green rocailles (lg brz-gr roc)

133 large sea-green rocailles (lg s-gr roc)

114 blue-green rocailles (bl-gr roc)

110 large green sand-blasted oblate beads (lg gr s-b ob bd)

9 5mm-diam dark green crystals (5m dk gr crs)

To make

1 Open out bag to smooth out drawstring gathers. At a side seam, make a concealed fastening-on stitch, then thread 1 bl-gr roc, 1 lg s-gr roc, 1 bl-gr roc, 1 6m iri gr-gld bg, 1 bl-gr roc, 3 gr-brz cut bd; pass needle down through bl-gr roc to form a picot of the 3 gr-brz cut bd, then thread 1 6m iri gr-gld bg, 1 bl-gr roc, 1 lg s-gr roc, 1 bl-gr roc.

2 Make a fastening-off stitch ¾" (2cm) along top edge and pass needle ¼" (5mm) along, sewing invisibly through folded fabric of top. Make a fastening-on stitch and repeat threading sequence (fig 1).

3 Continue by beading around top of bag, until you have completed 26 repeats in total, then between 1st and last repeat ¼" (5mm) gap, make a picot with 3 bl-gr roc, passing needle invisibly through fabric fold to come out close to 1st bl-gr roc of next repeat, thread 1 bl-gr roc, 1 6m iri gr-gld bg, 1 bl-gr roc, passing needle down into fabric fold, then repeat this sequence until you have completed each repeat (fig 2).

To work netting

1 Using a needle threaded with crochet thread, make a concealed fastening-on stitch and bring needle out to right side of bottom line of drawstring casing stitching, next to a side seam line.

2 Thread 1 lg brz-gr roc, 1 lg gr s-b ob bd, 1 lg brz-gr roc, and stitch into casing seam line 1" (2.5cm) along. Making a loop hanging ⅜" (1cm) approx from casing seam line, make a fastening-off stitch, bring needle back to right side of fabric close to the same point, and repeat this sequence until you reach 1st loop again (fig 3).

NB The casing is 22" (55cm) in circumference, and takes 22 repeats of loops; if your bag is a different size, adjust number of repeats as necessary.

3 Make a fastening-off stitch at beginning of 1st loop, and carefully stitch through 1st half of loop thread to secure (fig 4 opposite).

4 Take needle through 1st and 2nd bead on loop to begin to thread 2nd round. Allowing 1½" (3.5cm) of crochet thread per loop, multiply this by number of loops, and tie a contrasting color of thread at this measurement along the next length of thread you are using, so that when you reach end of 2nd round you can make sure your last fastening-off stitch is at this point, then stitch through thread again to begin 3rd round (fig 5 opposite).

5 Repeat instructions from steps 1–4 to work 4th and 5th round. Stitch through thread and knot at middle of ending loop, which will be concealed by middle

fig 3

fig 4

fig 5

bead. As long as you have the same length of thread for each round, a gentle shake will allow the beads to settle into loops of equal depth when all rounds are completed.

To work tassel finish

1 Fasten a strong piece of crochet thread, same color as velvet, to middle of bag base and, squeezing base tightly, begin to wrap thread around folds of fabric, decreasing in tightness as you wrap upward, stopping and finishing off at 1¼" (3cm) approx. This will form the beaded base above tassel (fig 6).

2 Measure 12 equal sections around wrapped base at widest point and mark with pins.

3 Using polyester thread, thread 1 6m iri gr-gld bg, 1 bl-gr roc, 1 6m iri gr-gld bg, 1 bl-gr roc, 3 gr-brz cut bd, pass needle back through the bl-gr roc to form a picot of the cut beads, then thread 1 6m iri gr-gld bg, 1 bl-gr roc, 1 6m iri gr-gld bg, stitch into base securely and pass needle back up through last bugle. Treating this as 1st bugle of previous sequence, continue until you have worked 12 beaded "points" (fig 7), which will form a flower-petal effect around base finish.

4 Between each of the "points" stitch a picot of bl-gr roc, and below these a round of vertical 6m iri gr-gld bg, to form a band (fig 8).

5 Continue to stitch rounds of b-gr roc picots, which will decrease in size to middle of bag base, and finish off neatly and securely.

6 Following basic beaded tassel instructions on page 43, make a 20-strand tassel of 30 2m gr-brz cut bg, ending with 15 gr-brz cut bd.

7 To make tassel head, thread on 1 b-gr roc, 1 5m dk gr crs, 1 b-gr roc, 1 lg s-gr roc, and stitch into end of beaded base. Make several fastening-off stitches into beaded base and cut off neatly.

To work drawstring cord finish

1 Gather velvet finish at the ends and stitch on 3 5m dk gr crs, with a beaded picot of bl-gr roc inbetween them (fig 9).

2 From center of crystals, thread 1 lg s-gr roc, 3 bl-gr roc, 1 5m dk gr crs, 1 bl-gr roc, 3 gr-brz cut bd, then pass needle up through the bl-gr roc to form a picot of the cut beads. Pass your thread through all other beads, and then finish off neatly and securely between the crystals.

fig 6

fig 7

fig 9

fig 8

51

beaded bags

Beads can add a pretty, personal touch to ready-made bags, such as the useful drawstring versions seen here. The plaid bag is finished with a stunning colorful trim worked in lime-green and yellow beads, while the rich velvet ruby bag has a glittering garnet and gold trim.

Beaded ends for the drawstring cords themselves add the final stylish finish.

Ruby bag

fig 1

fig 2

You will need

Velvet drawstring bag, 25″ (64cm) in circumference

4¾yd (4.5m) approx polyester thread, color matched to velvet

Needle fine enough to pass through smallest bead twice when threaded

888 small garnet cut beads (sm gnt cut bd)

544 small yellow cut beads (sm yel cut bd)

144 large iridescent garnet rocailles (lg iri gnt roc)

104 large iridescent gold rocailles (lg iri gld roc)

To make

1 Open out bag to smooth out drawstring gathers. Starting at one side seam line and using a concealed fastening-on stitch, bring needle out under bottom drawstring casing seam line on right side.

2 Thread 1 lg iri gld roc, 25 sm gnt cut bd, 1 lg iri gnt roc, 1 lg iri gld roc, 25 sm gnt cut bd, 1 lg iri gld roc.

3 Measuring 2½″ (6.5cm) along gather line, pass needle through to reverse side and make a fastening-off stitch, pass needle back toward fastening-on stitch by ¼″ (5mm) and bring it through to right side.

4 Thread 1 lg iri gnt roc, 16 sm yel cut bd, 1 lg iri gld roc, 1 lg iri gnt roc, 16 sm yel cut bd, 1 lg iri gnt roc, and pass through to reverse side ¼″ (5mm) from fastening-on stitch. Make a fastening-off stitch and bring needle through to right side of fabric ¼″ (5mm) to right of last stitch.

5 Thread 1 lg iri gld roc, 13 sm yel cut bd, 1 lg iri gnt roc, 1 lg iri gld roc, 1 lg iri gnt roc, 13 sm yel cut bd, 1 lg iri gnt roc, and stitch through to reverse side ¼″ (5mm) from last stitch. Make a fastening-off stitch and bring needle through to right side.

6 Thread 1 lg iri gnt roc, 6 sm yel cut bd, 1 lg iri gld roc, 1 lg iri gnt roc, 1 lg iri gld roc, 6 sm yel cut bd, 1 lg iri gnt roc. Pass needle through to reverse side ¼″ (5mm) from last stitch, make a few fastening-off stitches and cut off thread neatly (fig 1).

7 Starting again with a concealed fastening-on stitch at point A, repeat the sequence. Continue in this way around gather line until you have completed 10 repeats in total.

To finish

1 Pull drawstring cords to make them equal in length, and bind the pieces of cord together for each pull by whipping ends together as for the plaid bag (see fig 3 opposite), cutting off remaining cord neatly.

2 Make a large knot in the thread, then pass needle up through base of one of cord ends, and out through top of whipping. Thread 10 lg iri gnt roc and wrap them around cord, stitching through to anchor them. Bring needle out just below this round, thread another 10 lg iri gnt roc and repeat, then 2 more rounds of 10 lg iri gnt roc, making 4 rounds including 1st. Stitch across last round, and bring thread out of center point (fig 2).

3 Thread 20 sm gnt cut bd, 1 lg iri gld roc, 20 sm gnt cut bd, and stitch through base to make a loop. Thread 18 sm yel cut bd, 1 lg iri gnt roc, 18 sm yel cut bd, and stitch through base to make a loop. Thread 12 sm gnt cut bd, 1 lg iri gld roc, 12 sm gnt cut bd, and again make a loop; thread 8 sm yel cut bd, 1 lg iri gnt roc, 8 sm yel cut bd, and make another loop. This will form 4 loops, graduated in size (fig 3).

fig 3

Plaid bag

You will need

Plaid drawstring bag, 65" (164.5cm) in circumference
2.5m (2¾yd) polyester thread
Needle fine enough to pass through beads twice when threaded

428 lime-green rocailles (lim-gr roc)
84 large matt yellow rocailles (lg mt yel roc)
30 large purple sand-blasted oblate beads (lg pur s-b ob bd)

To make

1 Open out bag to smooth out drawstring gathers. Make a concealed fastening-on stitch: pass needle between turned-over fabric of top edge, from drawstring gathering line to top edge. Hold a tail of thread at drawstring line and make a few fastening-on stitches, ensuring that they are secure, and then pull thread tail a little and cut it off, so that tail slips invisibly into fabric fold (fig 1).
2 Using this secured thread, thread 1 lim-gr roc, 1 lg mt yel roc, 1 lg pur s-b ob bd, 1 lg mt yel roc, 6 lim-gr roc, 1 lg mt yel roc, 6 lim-gr roc, then pass needle up through 1st 4 beads threaded, make

fig 1

fig 2

a fastening-off stitch, and advance needle and thread invisibly 2½" (6cm) through fabric fold, make another fastening-off stitch. Repeat the sequence to make a loop (fig 2).
3 Continue in this way every 2½" (6cm) around top of bag, until you have 26 beaded loops.
NB The 2 bags used here both have plain cord endings. If the bag you are working on has a fabric tag attached, you can follow the instructions for the drawstring cord finish as for the evening bag seen in the photograph on page 51.

To finish

1 Pull drawstring cords to make them equal in length, and bind the pieces of cord together for each of the 2 pulls by whipping ends together, cutting off remaining cord neatly (fig 3).
2 Make a large knot in the thread and pass needle up through base of one of

fig 3

cord ends and out through top of whipping. Thread 4 lim-gr roc and pass needle back up through base.
3 Repeat this sequence 7 times more to form a beaded end, then from center of base thread 1 lg pur s-b ob bd, then the beaded loop sequence as for top edge (fig 4).
4 Finish off thread securely, and repeat for the other cord pull.

fig 4

beaded fringe

This is one of the simplest needle-threading techniques, and is a classic method exemplified in "Tiffany" style lampshades and the dresses of the 1920s "flappers," where the movement of the Charleston dance made the bead-fringed dresses shimmer in the light. The threading may be comparatively simple, but this technique creates a beautiful effect, especially when used as a lampshade, curtain, or blind edging, with light shining through the different qualities and colors of glass in the various beads.

Starting off

Beaded fringe can be worked by attaching each string of beads either directly to the object to be decorated or to a narrow fabric tape or ribbon, which is then itself applied to the object. If the fringe is to be worked onto a length of tape or ribbon, it is helpful to pin this to your cork board, moving the fringed length along as it is finished and re-pinning the next section to be worked, repeating this until the required length is completed. Whatever base the fringe is to be worked onto, the fringe-making techniques are the same. There are two main methods.

Making a long fringe

Here, the strings of beads are attached individually to form the fringe. Generally, this method would be used when working a long fringe; it is also the best method to use when applying a fringe to static objects, as opposed to clothing and accessories.

Ensuring the bead diameter is large enough to accommodate 4 thicknesses of polyester thread, work as follows:

1 Allow approx 6" (15cm) of thread over expected length of finished string, and double that measurement.
So, for a 20cm (8in) string:
(8"/20cm + 6"/15cm) x 2 = 28" (70cm) thread required

2 Double the thread and thread both ends into a needle. Sew ends through fringe base and through loop where thread is doubled, and pull tight (fig 1).

3 Thread on required number of beads, and pass needle back up through 2nd to last bead threaded, so that last bead forms end anchor. Make a fastening-off stitch with both threads between 2nd and 3rd to last beads (figs 2, 3, and 4).

4 Pass needle up to between 3rd and 4th last beads, and repeat fastening-off stitch.

5 Repeat this 2 or 3 times more, pulling fastening-off stitch tightly each time, and ensuring string of beads is hanging smoothly, not too tightly, and not so loosely that there is thread showing anywhere. To finish, tug the string of beads gently to ensure fastening-off is secure, and cut off remaining thread ends neatly (fig 5).

6 Move to next point where fringe is to be made, and repeat process until entire length of fringe is completed.

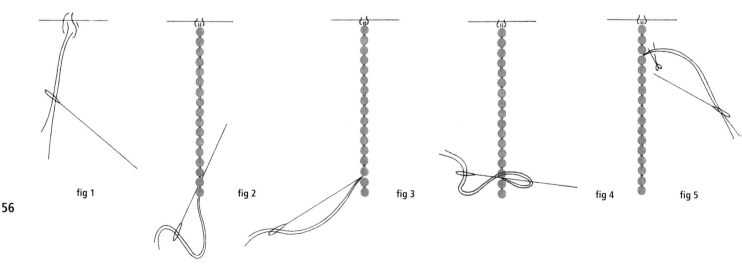

fig 1   fig 2   fig 3   fig 4   fig 5

fig 6

Making a short fringe

Here, the fringe is worked with one continuous thread through all the strings of beads (fig 6). This method is used when working a shorter length of fringe, as it is easier to keep the strings smooth and the beads hanging straight when passing the needle back up through a shorter length. Use it also when the bead diameter will only accommodate 2 thicknesses of thread. It is generally the best method to use for fringe applied to clothing or accessories, as here in the flecked-gauze bag with fringe, since there is no risk of the fastening-off stitches working loose with the movement of the fabric when worn, as they may do with the first method.

However, there are no hard-and-fast rules, so experiment.

The bag in the photograph has a fringe made of 49 strings of beads and bugles and approximately 5¼y (5m) of polyester thread.

1 To calculate quantity of thread needed, double length of each string and add one-third of total to allow for fastening-on and off.

2 When making a fringe over a short width, double thread quantity and tie it at center of fringed base.

3 Thread one end and work fringe from middle to side.

4 Thread other end and work whole length of thread for each string. Continue until fringing is complete.

You will find more ideas and instructions for designing and charting beaded fringe on page 106. It is also possible to create waved and other unusual profiles to the bottom edge of the fringe, so experiment with this interesting design possibility.

Bag with fringe

1 Pin the bag to a cork board, and divide bottom edge into 8 equal sections, marked with pins.
2 Pass threaded needle through bottom of bag at point A, leaving a short tail. Tie tail and working length together. The tail can either be threaded down 1st string of beads or stitched neatly into side seam when fringe is completed.
3 Working left to right from threading sequence chart (fig 7), thread on 2 iridescent green rocailles, 1 gold rocaille, 1 iridescent green rocaille, 1 leaf-green rocaille, 1 iridescent green rocaille, 1 leaf-green bugle, 1 leaf-green rocaille, 1 iridescent green rocaille, 1 gold rocaille and pass needle up through all rocailles threaded above last gold rocaille.
4 Continue threading and work to middle of chart (B) and from point B to D, making sure that all strings are equally spaced.
5 Repeat from A to C 3 more times between other pin points, remembering to add last string D at last pin point.
6 Pull thread firmly but not too tightly, as strings of beads and bugles should be fluid, not stiff.

NB It may be necessary to use more than one length of thread if you are making fringe over an extensive width.

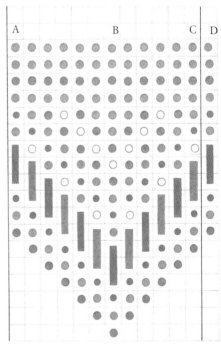

57

fig 7

lampshade cover

The beauty of fringe, whether worked in an intricate or a simple design, lies in the rich waterfall effect of beads hanging either closely side by side, or spaced as a fringe of long drops as in this lovely lampshade cover. Changing the color of the light bulb used in the lamp would enable you to transform the overall effect.

A   B

C   D

fig 1

You will need

Cream parchment lampshade,
34" (85cm) circumference x 5½" (14cm) deep
10" (25cm) cream organza,
45" (115cm) wide
10" (25cm) pale yellow dupioni silk,
115cm (45in) wide
Embroidery hoop or frame (optional)
Transparent nylon thread
Fine millener's or beading needle
Pale yellow sewing thread
Sewing needle
500 polished drilled rock crystals (rk crs)
350 4mm-diam clear glass faceted beads (4m fc bd)
75 6mm-diam clear glass faceted beads (6m fc bd)
35 clear glass pear-shaped drop bead (drp bd)

To prepare fabric

1 With right sides together, pin pale yellow dupioni silk to cream organza, then baste and machine stitch along one long edge. Press seam flat, and pink raw edges with pinking shears.
2 Open out joined fabrics right side up, and on cream organza mark 6" (15cm) from each edge, leaving a middle section of 34" (85cm), which will be the length to be beaded. Measure up ⅝" (2cm) from joining seam and make a basting line across width of organza – this is where the dense beading will be. Then from that line measure up 1¼" (3cm) and again make a basting line across width of organza – this is where the lighter beading will be (fig 1).

To work beading

1 Stretch joined fabric into a rectangular embroidery frame, or work sections along the width with organza part-mounted in a circular embroidery hoop, or carefully work the beading with fabric unstretched. If using a frame or hoop, make sure you keep grain (thread lines) of fabric straight to prevent it becoming distorted, which in turn will cause beading to be distorted when finished.
2 Begin by working ⅝" (2cm) border of dense beading. For every 4" (10cm) length, you will need 5 6m and 20 4m fd bd. Using the thread doubled, sew on beads randomly but evenly, filling in-between spaces with rk crs. Secure each of these with 2 stitches – one on either side – to keep it flat.
3 When dense beading is complete, work 1¼" (3cm) band of lighter beading. For every 4" (10cm) length, you will need 5 4m fc bd and approx 10 rk crs (as these are a natural stone the size varies, so use artistic license). Stitch on beads so that they appear to be lightly scattered onto the fabric. As thread is transparent, you can take it from bead to bead on reverse of fabric without finishing off each time.

To work fringe

1 Using a pencil, lightly mark every 1" (2.5cm) along seam line below dense beading area.
2 Count out beads for the fringe: for each fringe you will need 4 rk crs, 1 6m fc bd and 4 4m fc bd, and 1 drp bd.
3 Make 1 or 2 fastening-on stitches to fasten thread to 1st pencil mark. Thread 1 rk crs, 1 6m fc bd, 1 rk crs, 1 4m fc bd, 1 rk crs, 1 4m fc bd, 1 rk crs, 1 4m fc bd, 1 rk crs, 1 4m fc bd, 1 drp bd. Pass needle up through all beads and secure with 2 or 3 fastening-off stitches; then pass thread along back of fabric to next mark, and repeat with all fringes.

fig 2

To make

1 With right sides together, fold points A and B over to points C and D, then pin, baste and machine stitch with a 2cm (⅝in) seam allowance. Turn right side out and press down top seam. Make this "tube" into a circle: either machine stitch and press seam open, or turn under edges, butt together and stitch to join invisibly (fig 2).

2 Mark a line 3" (7.5cm) from top edge, by pinning around the circumference, and hand stitch a gathering thread along this line. Slip completed cover over cream parchment shade and pull gathers to fit top edge, ensuring that bottom edges of beaded cover and shade cover are lying together. Secure with 1 or 2 fastening-off stitches.

3 Punching needle carefully through parchment at approx 1¼" (3cm) intervals, sew beaded cover to shade.

59

Pin & wire beading

Pin beading involves using beads and/or sequins, and pins. It dates from the eighteenth and early nineteenth centuries, when pin-beaded pincushions or pinpillows were made to give as tokens of friendships and love. The cushions were tightly filled with sawdust or bran to provide a firm anchor for the pins. Today, the availability of compressed cushions and styrofoam shapes means you can easily pin bead little gifts or Christmas tree decorations, such as the baubles in this chapter.

Wire beading is the art of threading beads onto wire, then twisting them to create elegant shapes, like the colorful flowers and beautiful butterflies seen in this chapter. The craft is believed to date from as early as the fifteenth century and became particularly popular in Victorian England.

pin & wire beading

Pin-beaded patterns are suitable for small decorations such as glittering baubles and other festive decorations, while wire beading is ideal for creating naturalistic designs, such as those seen on pages 72–75, for example. The skill lies in the manipulation of the wired beads to create the required form. You might find it useful to follow a photograph or illustration – even real flowers – for reference.

Starting pin beading

In this technique, the beads and sequins are pinned into densely compressed cotton or styrofoam shapes or balls, using "lill" pins – short pins, ½" (14mm) long. If the base shape used is large it is possible to use ordinary dressmaking pins, but with smaller shapes you will need to use lill pins so that they do not cross over each other inside the base shape, making it difficult to push more pins in.

Unless you wish to paint the surface of the ball or cover it with fabric, it is best to pin closely to cover the surface completely. Depending on the desired effect, use beads only (fig 1), sequins only (fig 2), or both on one pin (fig 3). You can choose any combination of these, but if you choose beads only, you may need to color the surface of the ball first in a complementary color. Cup sequins, pinned concave side down, give a pleasing, smooth profile to the finished work.

When designing for a ball shape, it might be helpful to draw the ball on paper as an exploded shape – very like a flat representation of the world in an atlas. If this is drawn to scale, it can be glued to the ball and the design pinned through this into the ball, enabling you to work very complicated designs.

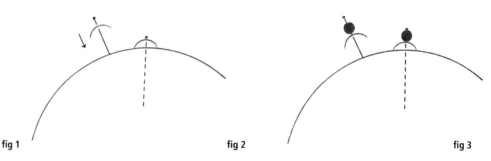

fig 1   fig 2   fig 3

Pin-beaded Christmas ball

When working pin beading, hold the bead shape either in one hand while you work the pinning with the other, or, if you prefer to have both hands free, scrunch up some tissue paper to make a "nest" in which to rest the shape, turning it as you work. It is best to pin in the color that is to be least dominant – the background color – first and then pin shape outlines overlapping this, to give a definite line to the design. This will enable you to create different intensities and subtleness of color.

1 Choose mother-of-pearl cup sequins in dark brown, orange, bronze, and red. Use a small compressed cotton ball for the shape.
2 Draw the design onto the ball using a felt-tip pen.
3 Pin the top of the ball with mother-of-pearl cup sequins, inserted very close together and pinning sequins concave side down.

4 Pin on dark brown cup sequins, interspersed with orange, bronze, and red cup sequins.
5 Finish by adding a small looped bow, decorated with sequin leaves and red beads to give a holly-berry effect, attached by 2 dressmaking pins. If you insert the pins at an angle they will not pull out when the ball is suspended as a tree ornament or hanging ornament.

Starting wire beading

This technique basically consists of threading beads onto fine wire and twisting the wire to secure the beads.

Materials suitable for wire beading include silver- or gold-colored electrical, craft, or beading wires. Fishing equipment stores are another good source, as they sell many different colors of fine wire which are used by fishermen to tie fishing flies. The wire might seem attractive enough to leave unwrapped, but the traditional finish to a flower stem is to wrap it with green silk floss. With a little practice this process can be completed quite quickly, and is useful if the bead flower is attached to a stem made of thicker wire, as the joint will be disguised.

Experiment by varying the different sizes and color combinations of the beads in order to achieve a realistic effect, or work entirely from your intuition and imagination, and see what you can create.

Wire beaded flower

Choose beads to match the colors of your chosen design. Use either solid or transparent rocailles to vary the effect. Use bugles or rocailles for the stamens and green silk floss for covering the wire stem.

1 Take 12" (30cm) of wire. Bend in half and thread 9 rocailles onto one end of wire. Push up to the bend.

2 Twist wire together, below loop of beads (fig 1). Thread on another 9 rocailles on one end and twist together (fig 2).

3 On the other end thread on 9 rocailles and twist again (fig 3). Repeat again with each end (fig 4). When you have 5 petals, twist ends securely together. Take one end of the wire and pass it

fig 6　　　　　fig 7

through the petals to the center of the flower.

4 Thread on one yellow rocaille to form stamen in the middle of the flower (fig 5).

5 Push end of wire back down to join other end and twist together.

6 Cover wire stem by wrapping with green silk floss (figs 6 and 7).

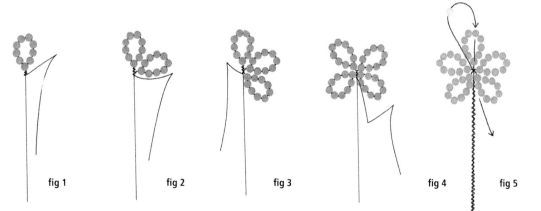

fig 1　　　　fig 2　　　　fig 3　　　　fig 4　　　　fig 5

Making a bouquet

To create a bouquet effect you could make several flowers, and wire them all together as a bunch, varying the length of the stems as if arranging a real bouquet. Tying them with a decorative ribbon, finished with a bow covering the wiring, would complete the final arrangement.

embellished tassels

Wire beading is a versatile technique which you can apply to many different facets of home decoration. These wire-beaded flowers make gorgeously decorative tassels and tie-backs that will enhance any home.

Gold roses and pearls

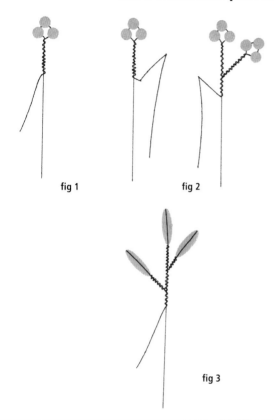

fig 1

fig 2

fig 3

You will need

Pink silky tassel, 5" (12cm) long approx
7 gold fabric roses
Spool of fine wire
Gold spray craft paint
Cork board and plastic sheet
100 (approx) seed pearls
50 (approx) round pearls, 3mm and
    6mm diameter

To make

1 To assemble sprays of wired round pearls, cut a piece of wire 16" (40cm) long approx and bend it in half. Thread on 3 3mm round pearls, push up to the bend and twist wire several times below them, forming a picot (fig 1).

2 Take one end of wire and bend approx ¾" (2cm). Thread on 3 more 3mm round pearls and push up to this point, then twist to join main stem. Twist stem together several times (fig 2).

3 Using longer length of wire, repeat sequence with another 3 3mm round pearls. Continue in this way, varying length of side branches.

4 Repeat steps 1–3 to make another spray, but using only single seed pearls (fig 3).

5 Make several more sprays, varying finished lengths, and incorporating some 6mm round pearls with the 3mm round pearls.

6 Push finished sprays into a cork board protected with a plastic sheet, and spray with gold craft paint.

7 When dry, push each spray into base of tassel head, bend back to stem, twist to secure. Work all around base of tassel head, alternating lengths of sprays.

8 To finish, glue 7 fabric roses evenly around base of tassel head, concealing where sprays are attached.

Pearl and crystal flowers

You will need

Cream tassel, 6" (15cm) circumference at base of tassel head
Spool of fine gold-colored wire
Cream polyester thread
Sewing needle
500 2mm rainbow crystal cut bugles (2m rbw crs bg)
250 2mm-diam round pearls (2m rnd pl)
20 6mm baroque pearls (6m prl)
20 3mm rainbow crystal cut bugles (3m rbw crs bg)
8 4mm-diam rainbow faceted crystals (4m rbw fc crs)
7 1cm-diam round pearls (1cm rnd prl)
7 7mm-diam round pearls (7m rnd prl)

To make pearl flower

1 For each flower petal, carefully cut a piece of wire 16" (40cm) long. Bend in half and thread on 3 2m rnd prl. Bend to form a picot and pass right-hand end of wire through 1st 2 pearls threaded (fig 1).

fig 1

fig 2

2 Pull these close together, thread 3 2m rnd prl onto left-hand end of wire and bend toward right side (fig 2).
3 Pass right-hand end of wire through pearls toward left side. Repeat sequence with a row of 4 and then 5 2m rnd pl, then decrease using 4, then 3, then 2, then 1, to complete the petal (fig 3). Make 4 more petals identically.
4 To make the stamens, cut a piece of wire 6" (15cm) long approx, bend it in half, thread on a 6m prl and twist wire for about ¾" (2cm) to form the stamen.

fig 3

Repeat these instructions to make 9 more identical stamens.
5 Twist the 10 stamen stems together, and grouping petals realistically around them, twist all together to form a convincing bead flower.

To make crystal flowers

1 Make 20 petals as for pearl flower, but using 2m rbw crs bg instead of 2m rnd prl.
2 Make 20 stamens using a single 3m rbw crs bg, and 8 stamens using a single 4m rbw fc crs.
3 Assemble 3 flowers, 2 with 5 petals and 10 3m rbw crs bg stamens, and 1 with 10 petals and 8 4m rbw fc crs stamens. Group all 5 flowers together so that the large crystal flower hangs below the 2 pearl flowers, with a crystal flower to either side of pearl flowers, and twist stems together to form a spray of flowers.
4 Using cream polyester thread, stitch 7 1cm rnd prl and 7 7m rnd prl alternately around base of tassel head. Position spray of flowers above this row of pearls and stitch securely into tassel head. Bend petals out gently.

Old roses and pearls

You will need

Large soft pink tassel tie-back, 10" (25cm) circumference at base of tassel head
6 old rose paper roses with paper leaves, 1½" (3.5cm) diameter
Fabric glue
Pale pink strong thread
Sewing needle
16 4mm-diam pale pink round pearls
12 5mm-diam pale pink round pearls
7 1cm-diam round pearls

To make

1 Using pale pink strong thread, stitch pearls to tassel head in order to create a random scattered effect, alternating bead sizes.
2 Pin paper roses around base of tassel head, spacing them evenly to create a natural effect.
3 Attach roses to tassel head securely using fabric glue.

Gold bow and pearls

You will need

Large cream cotton tassel tie-back, 12" (30cm) circumference at base of tassel head
Spool of fine gold-colored wire
Cream polyester thread; sewing needle
1 pearl and 2 crystal 5-petalled flowers, made as for pearl and crystal flowers

To make

1 Make 10 tiny tassels using pale pink embroidery thread, by making equal bundles of 2" (5cm) lengths and tying them at their centers. Bend each bundle in half, smooth down, and wrap more pale pink embroidery thread around the bunch ¼" (5mm) from center tie.
2 Stitch 5 fabric flowers around tassel head and stitch completed tassel to end of one of main tassel strands. Repeat with other 9 tiny tassels, dotting them among the strands evenly, or stitching a strand into a loop and attaching a tiny tassel to the loop end.

20" (50cm) gold gauze wired ribbon
Pearl-covered jewelry mount
25 small pink-and-white fabric flowers
25 small yellow-and-white fabric flowers
Pale pink embroidery cotton
250 (approx) crystal rocailles
250 (approx) rainbow crystal drop beads

3 Make approx 16 long drops of alternating rainbow crystal drop beads and crystal rocailles. They should be long enough to hang below main tassel by 1¾–2" (4–5cm). Stitch drops to inside of tassel strands.
4 Make other shorter drops and stitch around base of tassel head.
5 Form a bow from gold gauze ribbon and stitch the pearl-covered mount, or a clump of tied pearls, to its center. Stitch this to base of tassel head, with a crystal flower to either side of it.
6 Push pearl flower into top of tassel head above bow. Twist wire to secure.

Rainbow crystals and pearls

You will need

Small cream tassel, approx 4" (10cm) long, encircled by 8 smaller tassels
305 2mm rainbow crystal cut bugles
120 3mm-diam round pearls

To make

1 Make 5 petals as for the pearl and crystal flowers, using 2mm rainbow crystal cut bugles.
2 Make 5 larger petals, using 36 bugles instead of 25.
3 Make 8 stamens using 4mm-diam rainbow faceted crystals, and 6 stamens using a single crystal rocaille for each.
4 Assemble the flower by grouping the 5 smaller petals around the bunch of stamens, and the 5 larger petals around the smaller petals. Twist all stems together and cut so that only ⅜" (1cm) of main stem remains. Push this into tassel head and stitch to secure.
5 Using 2 rainbow faceted crystals and 9 3mm-diam round pearls per drop in sequence shown (fig 4), stitch a 1cm-long pear-shaped pearl drop bead to

16 4mm-diam rainbow faceted crystals
6 crystal rocailles
4 1cm-long pear-shaped pearl drop beads

base of tassel head of every alternate small tassel. Stitch 7 3mm-diam round pearls across top and base of tassel heads to finish.

fig 4

pin-beaded baubles

Here one basic shape is used to create three different designs. You could also adapt the idea to make Easter eggs or even a mobile for a child's room. All quantities of sequins given in the materials listed here are approximate.

Star bauble

You will need

Compressed cotton ball, 2½"
   (60mm) diameter
1¼oz (35g) approx gold-colored lill pins
⅓oz (10g) approx silver-colored lill pins
160 5mm-diam rainbow turquoise-blue
   cup sequins
160 5mm-diam rainbow pale blue
   cup sequins
70 5mm-diam silver cup sequins
40 tiny gold star sequins
30 silver pointed oval-shaped sequins
25 small silver star sequins
2 large turquoise rocailles
2 5mm-diam pale blue faceted beads

To make

Use silver-colored lill pins for all sequins except tiny gold stars, when gold-colored pins should be used.

1 Mark ball into halves. At center of line on one "side," make a star using silver pointed oval-shaped sequins (fig 1).

2 Fill gap left in center with a small silver star sequin. Pin in a tiny gold star sequin at each of the 5 angles of star, and 4 around central silver star sequin. Repeat at midpoint of opposite line, so that there is a "front" and a "back" star.

3 Outline stars with 5mm-diam rainbow turquoise-blue cup sequins, and then work 3 or 4 rounds of same sequins from this, pinning them unevenly on outer round and interspersing with 5mm-diam rainbow pale blue and 5mm-diam silver cup sequins. Complete the "sky" with patches of 5mm-diam rainbow pale blue and silver cup sequins, and scatterings of tiny gold and small silver stars.

4 To finish, make a looped bow, using large turquoise rocailles and 5mm-diam pale blue faceted beads, to secure.

fig 1

Moon bauble

You will need

Compressed cotton ball, 2½"
(6cm) diameter

12" (30cm) approx dark blue satin
ribbon, ⅜" (1cm) wide

1oz (30g) approx gold-colored lill pins

½oz (15g) approx silver-colored lill pins

250 6mm-diam deep blue cup sequins

100 5mm-diam deep blue cup sequins

100 5mm-diam silver cup sequins

100 5mm-diam rainbow smoky
transparent cup sequins

40 5mm-diam rainbow transparent
cup sequins

20 small silver star sequins

2 large silver rocailles

2 5mm-diam deep blue faceted beads

Tracing paper

To make

1 Mark ball into quarters, like orange segments. If this is difficult to gauge freehand, slip an elastic band around ball to divide it in half, slip on another at right angles to this one, and then draw carefully alongside bands using a soft pencil.

2 Trace moon pattern (fig 1) and cut out. Carefully pin tracing paper moon at midpoint of one quarter line on ball, slanting it backward slightly, and draw around it using a soft pencil (fig 2). Repeat this at midpoint of opposite quarter line, so that ball has a "front" and a "back" moon.

3 Using silver-colored lill pins, pin bead moons by first pinning inside the shapes using 5mm-diam rainbow transparent cup sequins (fig 3).

4 Using silver-colored lill pins and 5mm-diam silver cup sequins, fill in and outline moon shapes, pinning into drawn line for outline. Now draw a line between moons, looping to either side of other circle line (fig 4).

5 Using silver-colored lill pins, pin along looping line using 5mm-diam rainbow smoky transparent cup sequins, adding a 5mm-diam silver cup sequin after every 3rd or 4th rainbow transparent cup sequin.

6 Using gold-colored lill pins, pin 5mm-diam deep blue cup sequins around moons. Then fill in the "sky," using a combination of 5mm- and 6mm-diam deep blue cup sequins – the different sequin sizes can reflect color quite differently and will give added depth to the sky.

7 Using silver-colored lill pins, pin a single small silver star sequins into the sky at random intervals, to give a scattered star effect.

8 To finish, cut ends of ribbon at a slant to prevent it from unraveling and form the ribbon into a looped bow, securing each loop end with a dressmaking pin with the addition of a large silver rocaille, 5mm-diam deep blue faceted bead, and silver star sequin.

NB If using as a tree decoration, pin ribbon bow in at top of sky, at a slant to prevent pins pulling out when ball is suspended by the loop (see photograph page 62).

fig 1

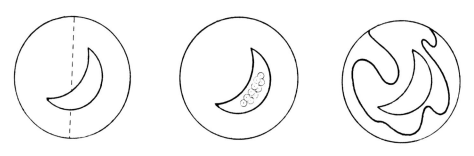

fig 2   **fig 3**   **fig 4**

Sun bauble

You will need

Compressed cotton ball, 2½"
  (60mm) diameter
1oz (25g) approx gold-colored lill pins
¾oz (20g) approx silver-colored lill pins
360 3mm-diam gold flat sequins
300 5mm-diam brilliant sky-blue
  cup sequins
40 5mm-diam bronze cup sequins
25 5mm-diam rainbow cream-pink
  cup sequins
2 large iridescent bronze rocailles
2 5mm-diam bronze metallic
  faceted beads
Tracing paper

To make

Use gold-colored lill pins for pinning the
sun, and silver-colored lill pins for the
"sky."
1 Mark ball into 2 halves using method
described for the Moon bauble. Trace
sun pattern (fig 1) and cut out.
2 Pin tracing paper sun at midpoint of
line on one "side" and draw around it
using a soft pencil. Repeat this at
midpoint of opposite line, so that ball
has a "front" and a "back" sun.

3 Pin a circle of 5mm-diam bronze cup
sequins into center of sun. Pin 5mm-
diam rainbow cream-pink cup sequins
into left curve, and fill in rest of center
with 5mm-diam bronze cup sequins
(fig 2).

fig 2

4 Outline sun shape by pinning 3mm-
diam gold flat sequins onto drawn line.
Fill in north, south, east, and west sun
flares solidly with same sequins (fig 1).
5 Pin 5mm-diam rainbow cream-pink
cup sequins into central part of other 4
flares, and a 5mm-diam bronze cup
sequin at base of each; then complete
with 3mm-diam gold flat sequins.
6 Using 5mm-diam brilliant sky-blue cup
sequins, complete sky by filling between
the suns.
7 To finish, make a looped bow as for
the Moon bauble, using large iridescent
bronze rocailles and 5mm-diam bronze
metallic faceted beads to secure.

Instead of finishing with a bow, try
decorating the bauble with the other
beading techniques you have mastered,
perhaps finishing with a tassel or a wire-
beaded flower, for example. You could
also experiment making several balls
with the same motif but in different
sizes. Alternative bauble designs can be
found on page 106.

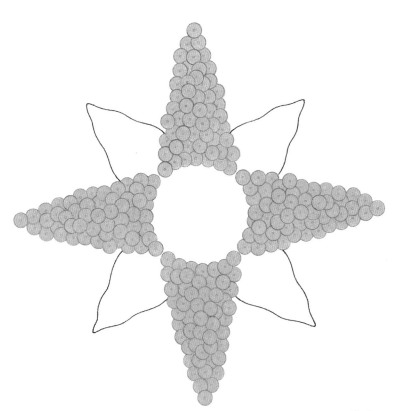

fig 1

wire-beaded flowers

Wire-beading was particularly popular in Venice in the eighteenth century when gondolas, altars, and domestic interiors were traditionally decorated with wire-beaded flowers. Here basic flower and leaf designs are used for a variety of decorative items – to form the basis of a pretty posy which would look lovely as a dining table centerpiece or resting on a mantelpiece, to grace a highly original hatpin and to embellish a brooch to make a fetching floral corsage.

Forget-me-not posy

You will need
Spool of wire and green silk floss
Spool of thicker wire 20cm (8in) long
300 approx of following rocailles:
Dark green transparent (dk gr trs roc)
Lime-green transparent (lim-gr trs roc)
Red transparent (rd trs roc)
Pink-lined transparent (pk-lnd trs roc)
Blue-lined transparent (bl-lnd trs roc)
Pale turquoise (ple turq roc)
Yellow (yel roc)
Pearl (prl roc)
200 approx of following 2mm cut bugles:
Pale blue (2m ple bl cut bg)
Red (2m rd cut bg)
Dark green (2m dk gr cut bg)
Pearly-white (2m prl-wh cut bg)

fig 1

To make
1 Using 6 2m dk gr cut bg per branch, make 1 14-branch and 2 12-branch leaf sprays, following step 6 of the hatpin instructions on page 74.
2 Using 7 dk gr trs roc per branch, make 3 7-branch and 3 8-branch leaf sprays, as described on page 74.
3 Using 7 lim-gr trs roc per branch, make 1 7-branch, 1 8-branch, and 2 11-branch leaf sprays, as described.
4 Make 2 loops of 90 lim-gr trs roc, twist together at their centers and pinch together to make long tulip-like leaves (fig 1).
5 Repeat step 4 twice more, then make 3 more leaves using dk gr trs roc.
6 Following figs 1–5 on page 63, make 9 forget-me-not flowers using ple turq roc and 1 yel roc for each center.
7 Make 12 similar flowers using pk-lnd trs roc, 6 using bl-lnd trs roc, and 3 using rd trs roc. Make 2 similar but 4-

petalled flowers, using 2m ple bl cut bg.
8 Following step 2 of the corsage instructions on page 75, make 5 3-leaf sprays using dk gr trs roc, and 3 3-leaf sprays using lim-gr trs roc.
9 Using dk gr trs roc make a fern-type leaf following steps shown in fig 2.
10 Make 14 more fern-type leaves using dk gr trs roc, and 12 similar leaves using lim-gr trs roc. Twist together 3 of the same color, to make a 3-branch spray.
11 Form a red rose petal by making rounds of 11, 15, 19, 23, 27, and 31 rd trs roc, working from inside loop outward. Repeat 3 times to make a total of 4 petals. Work 3 smaller petals for center, and 5 single loops of 9 beads each for stamens.
Repeat once more, and make 1 similar using 2m rd cut bg.
12 Make 3 3-petal flowers, using rounds of 20, 25, and 30 prl roc per petal, and 3 stamens, each of a loop of 12 yel roc.

fig 2

fig 3

13 To make butterflies, work top wings following fig 3 and using the same technique as for flower petals on page 66. Work bottom wings by following fig 3, but this time intertwine each row with top wing.

14 Make butterfly body following fig 4.

15 To complete butterfly, slip wire ends of wings into side wires of body, thread back inside beads and cut off neatly.

16 Take each finished piece of posy and twist it to a length of thicker wire for the stem, then cover with green silk

floss as shown in figs 6–7 on page 63. Finish bouquet as described on page 63.

17 Position butterflies as though they had just flown to rest on the posy.

fig 4

Hatpin

You will need

Hatpin stalk with point protector
Pear-shaped compressed cotton shape
16yd (15m) approx wire and green
   silk floss
Bodkin or stiletto (for piercing)
Gold craft paint or spray
Craft glue
80 approx of following rocailles:

Dark green transparent (dk gr trs roc)
Lime-green transparent (lim-gr trs roc)
Red transparent (rd trs roc)
Pale turquoise (ple turq roc)
Yellow (yel roc)
50 2mm pale blue-lined cut bugles
   (ple bl-lnd cut bg)
50 2mm pink-lined cut bugles
   (pk-lnd cut bg)

To make

1 Make a ⅛" (3mm) diameter hole in rounded end of pear shape, by pushing in a bodkin or stiletto about ⅝" (1.5cm) deep. Paint or spray pear shape using gold craft paint and leave to dry.

2 Make 3 5-petalled forget-me-nots, by threading on 9 ple turq roc and twisting to make 1 petal (figs 1–5 on page 63).

3 Make 1 similar flower, using 9 pk-lnd cut bg per petal, and 1 yel roc for stamen. Make 2 more flowers, with only 4 petals, using ple bl-lnd cut bg, 9 per petal, and 1 pk-lnd cut bg for stamen.

4 Make 1 similar 5-petalled flower, using 13 red transparent rocailles per

petal. Twist wire stem tight and cut to ¾" (2cm), coat this with craft glue and push down into top of pear shape.

5 Twist stems of the 1 pink and 2 pale blue flowers tight and cut to ¼" (5mm). Coat with craft glue and push into pear shape halfway down, spacing flowers around circumference.

6 Using 7 dk gr trs roc per branch, make a 5-branched spray as shown in fig 1.

7 Make another spray of dk gr trs roc, 2 sprays of lim-gr trs roc , and 1 spray with branches 1, 4, and 5 of dark green, and branches 2 and 3 of lim-gr trs roc.

8 Cover spray stems with green silk floss (see figs 6–7, page 63).

9 Put craft glue into hole in base of pear shape and insert sprays, spacing them around circumference of pear. Cover ¾" (2cm) of 2 of forget-me-not stems with green silk floss and insert these into hole. Now insert hatpin stalk into center of wires and hole, and push a forget-me-not next to it, so that petals of flower nestle around stalk and hatpin appears to be coming out of center.

10 Bend sprays over pear shape.

fig 1

Corsage

You will need

Large brooch or tie pin
Dark green metal claw-mounted
  embroidery stone
Spool of wire and green silk floss
100 approx of following rocailles:
Dark green transparent (dk gr trs roc)
Lime-green transparent (lim-gr trs roc)
Red transparent (rd trs roc)

Pink-lined transparent (pk-lnd trs roc)
Pale turquoise (ple turq roc)
Yellow (yel roc)
White (wh roc)
Gold metallic (gld met roc)
Pearl (prl roc)
60 2mm pale blue cut bugles
  (ple bl cut bg)

To make

1 Make 6 individual leaves, using rounds of 8, 18, and 28 dk gr trs roc, pinch at top to make a leaf shape (fig 1).

fig 1

2 Make 1 3-leaf spray using same leaf (fig 2).

3 Make 3 5-petalled forget-me-nots (see technique on page 63). Make 2 similar flowers using pk-lnd trs roc, each with 1 yel roc and 1 ple turq roc for stamen.

4 Using same number of beads per round as for dark green leaves, make 1 4-petalled flower using rd trs roc, leaving wire rounded. Make 1 flower as forget-me-not using gld met roc with a

prl roc picot center. Twist this with red flower, to make gold flower its center.

5 Repeat instructions making 1 4-petalled flower of ple bl cut bg with a "forget-me-not" center of gld met roc.

6 Form a flower from 9 loops of rd trs roc and 9 loops of wh roc (fig 3). Continue twisting together.

7 Following fig 1 of the hatpin shown opposite, make 2 5-branched leaf sprays of 7 dk gr trs roc each, 1 spray of lim-gr trs roc, and 1 spray of mixed gr trs roc.

8 Make 3 loops of 7 rd trs roc, following fig 3, and repeat once.

9 Cover all stems with green silk floss (see figs 6–7 on page 63). Lay leaf sprays and flowers together, as if arranging a tiny bouquet, varying the lengths. Twist all together and, leaving approx ⅝" (1.5cm) of wrapped stems protruding over one end of the pin, bind to the brooch or tie pin with wire, then wrap green silk floss over this.

10 To finish, attach the embroidery stone to center of 1 dark green leaf, carefully bend out flower petals, and arrange the sprays as required.

fig 2

fig 3

75

Bead embellishments

Beads can add richness and texture when used to embellish the surface of a fabric, either as an abstract adornment or to represent and to emphasize a feature of a natural form, such as the needlepoint blue poppy pillow and the beaded strawberry and pear designs seen in this chapter. Beads can also be incorporated to beautiful effect with other textile crafts, where they form an integral part of the technique. An example of this is the original cloche and mittens design, where knitting and beading combine with dramatic results.

surface beading

Beads and sequins are a highly versatile method of embellishment. You can use them to decorative effect on many furnishing fabrics – from felt and chintz to velvet and silk. Adding beads as an ornamental touch to a completed needlepoint design can also be attractive. Further, beads can be combined with many other craft techniques, such as crochet or bobbin lace. Here are just a few ideas, but you could try experimenting with any of your favorite textile techniques.

Bead embroidery

There are two methods of using beads or sequins as an embellishment to the surface of a fabric. They can either be combined with other thread embroidery techniques or simply stitched on. This idea has already been explored in miniature with the beaded buttons on pages 44–47; in this chapter it has been employed to decorate three-dimensional "beaded fruits," representing and emphasizing the fruits' features.

These themes can be developed further by applying beads to a textured ground fabric, such as a damask or tapestry weave, with the beads used to enhance the fabric design. With a plain fabric the embroidered beads may form the dominant feature, but when they are incorporated with a textured fabric usually each will enhance the inherent qualities of the other. To design and work both the ground fabric and the beading can present exciting and challenging possibilities, as shown in the pillow on page 82, where the poppy characteristics are perfect for embellishing with beading.

Beading on finished needlepoint

When using beads or sequins to decorate completed needlepoint designs, such as the pillow on page 82, it is best to pick colors that will contrast with the stitching. When choosing the size of the beads, take into consideration the end use: on a pillow, for instance, it might prove better to use small beads which will nestle into the wool of the needlepoint, bugles which will follow the direction of the stitched background, or even Japanese magatamas, rather than large beads which could prove a little uncomfortable.

1 Use tent stitch to cover the background (fig 1). When starting off, leave a long loose end of yarn at back of canvas and work first few stitches from right to left over it. Work following row of stitches below last row. Continue working alternately from right to left, then from left to right (fig 2).
2 When starting a new thread next to an area that has already been stitched, simply run thread through the back of a few stitches to secure and then bring needle out to front of needlepoint at position required.
3 To attach a bead when a needlepoint is completed, use strong sewing thread to match bead and a needle fine enough to pass through bead hole. Fasten on by using a large knot or making one or two fastening-on stitches on back of canvas. Stitch into place.
4 Fasten off neatly on back of canvas.

fig 1

fig 2

Beading on fabric

To create the decorative effect used in the beaded pear and strawberry seen on pages 85–87, choose sequins and beads to complement the fabric and to represent the natural features of the fruits.

You could also use this technique to add extra texture to soft furnishing accessories such as pillows and bolsters.

1 Cut a length of sewing thread and pull it several times through a small block of beeswax for ease of working.
2 Make a large knot, bring needle through fabric to the point where you wish to position a sequin, and thread on a sequin.
3 Thread on a bead of your choice, then pass needle back down through sequin hole so that bead is anchoring sequin to fabric. Make a few fastening-off stitches on reverse side of fabric and cut off thread neatly.
4 Repeat this sequence with all sequins until you have achieved your desired decorative effect. You can experiment by varying the color combination of beads and sequins.

For more ideas for combining beading with other embroidery techniques, see the information on couching on page 80. Beading can also be combined with appliqué, as with the denim shirt design on page 94.

Bead knitting

Beads can add an extra dimension to knitting. You can bead a motif, integrating beads into the knitting pattern, as with the cloche and mittens on page 88–93. You can also add beads as a finishing touch, as with the picot edging in the same pattern. Always consider the end use of the knitted item, being careful not to add beads where it would be impractical.

If incorporating beads into a knitting pattern, careful charting of your design is essential, so that you can accurately thread your chosen beads onto your working yarn. If you are knitting a large area or using heavy beads, be prepared to thread only as many beads as you need for the first one or two rows in order to minimize the possibility of breaking the yarn.

In bead knitting, the best way of guaranteeing success is always to slip a stitch (fig 1) before pushing up a bead to the work (fig 2). This ensures that the bead will lie neatly across the front of the knitting and will not slip through to the reverse side of the finished article.

fig 1

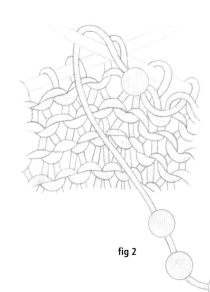

fig 2

Other surface beading

In the same way that beads can be incorporated with knitting, they can be also be integrated into other craft techniques. The pattern on pages 88–93 could be adapted to crochet, for example. With bead crochet, as with bead knitting, charting and threading are the most important criteria. You could either thread the beads onto the crochet thread or yarn and pass them gently up the working yarn when required, or, if the bead hole diameter is large enough to accommodate the crochet hook, hook the beads individually when they are required.

Beads can also be incorporated while working on canvas, as a beaded motif with a tent stitch background, for instance, in which case the beads are stitched to the canvas first, using doubled cotton sewing thread or single polyester thread and the background is worked once the beads are in place. Alternatively, beads and thread can be used for each tent stitch, resulting in a totally beaded canvas. It is important to consider the use of the finished needlepoint when deciding which method to apply.

Beads and bobbin lace are another effective combination. Here the beads are threaded first, usually onto the same yarn as that used for the lace, and wound onto a separate bobbin. This is then worked into the lace pattern using only the yarn until a bead is required, when the bead is pushed up to the right position, the bobbins twisted and the bead bobbin used for the yarn only until the next bead required.

Couched beading

An interesting way to use surface beading is to decorate a printed or woven motif with beads, and then appliqué the beaded motif to another fabric. This is the technique used for the project on pages 94–96, in which a printed blue-and-white plate and fruit dish motif has been beaded and then applied to a blue denim shirt, to striking effect.

The method used to attach the beads to the motif is called "couching." Couching is used for certain beaded designs, as it produces a smoother profile and better linear effect than stitching down each bead individually through its hole. By pushing the beads close together on the thread being couched, you will be able to achieve a more continuous line than when stitching them individually.

Couching is an embroidery technique often used to apply a thread or yarn that is too thick to be stitched into the fabric ground; instead, it is held to the fabric by "couching" it down with a finer thread. Bead couching is worked as follows.

1 Lay down a pre-strung length of beads to follow design line.
2 Stitch over this thread using a separate, finer thread, working stitches over thread between beads (figs 1–3).

3 After couching down each bead, slide next one up close to it, and couch down thread between that bead and the next.

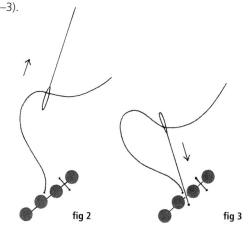

fig 1   fig 2   fig 3

Couched leaf This leaf design is a simple motif that would look striking stitched as a repeat motif on a plain fabric such as damask, although any firmly woven fabric would be suitable. You could use it to make a tablecloth, for example, complemented by matching napkins. Alternatively, you could use it on an item of clothing, such as a vest or a pocket.

1 Draw leaf design onto fabric and then mount in an embroidery hoop or frame – it is difficult to avoid puckering if couching unstretched fabric.

2 Thread 16" (40cm) approx polyester thread, make a fastening-on stitch and bring needle through to front of fabric at B in fig 1. Thread on 25 dark green rocailles (dk gr roc).

3 Thread another needle with 20" (50cm) approx sewing thread, make a fastening-on stitch, then bring needle through to front of fabric, one bead length up center leaf vein line from B.

4 Pulling bead thread taut, stitch ("couch") down over it with sewing thread, then advance needle below fabric one more bead length up center leaf vein line.

5 Repeat step 4, following drawn line carefully and pulling bead thread taut each time, as far as A. Thread both needles one after the other through stitches on reverse of fabric as far as C.

6 Bring bead thread needle through to front of fabric at right-hand side of center leaf vein line, and thread approx 50 leaf-green rocailles (lf-gr roc).

7 Bring sewing thread needle to front of fabric one bead length down outside leaf line. Working as before, couch down this line as far as D. Thread both needles one after the other through stitches on reverse of fabric as far as B.

8 Working as before, couch up outside leaf line as far as C, adding more lf-gr roc to bead thread if necessary, or slipping off any excess.

9 Bring bead thread needle through to front of fabric, one half bead width below outside leaf line on right of center leaf vein line and close to it. Then bring sewing thread needle through to front of fabric, one bead length below bead thread.

10 Next work 13 short filling-in rows from C to B down right-hand side of leaf. Thread 5 dk gr roc and 1 lf-gr roc onto bead thread, then couch down with sewing thread following curve of outside leaf line.

11 Bring both needles through to front of fabric at E. Thread 6 lf-gr roc onto bead thread and couch up to center leaf vein line again, following curve of last line couched.

12 Continue down leaf in this way, threading and couching down each row as follows: 5 dk gr roc and 1 lf-gr roc; 7 lf-gr roc; 5 dk gr roc and 1 lf-gr roc; 7 lf-gr roc; 4 dk gr roc and 2 lf-gr roc; 6 lf-gr roc; 3 dk gr roc and 3 lf-gr roc; 5 lf-gr roc; 3 dk gr roc and 2 lf-gr roc; 4 lf gr roc; 1 dk gr roc and 3 lf-gr roc.

13 Bring both needles through to front of fabric just above B. Working toward and away from center leaf vein line alternately, and filling in upward toward C, thread and couch down each row as follows: 3 lf-gr roc; 2 dk gr roc; 5 lf gr roc; 7 dk gr roc and 1 leaf-gr roc; 8 lf-gr roc; 7 dk gr roc and 1 lf-gr roc; 9 lf-gr roc; 8 dk gr roc and 1 lf-gr roc. Make 1 or 2 fastening-off stitches on reverse side of fabric and cut off threads neatly.

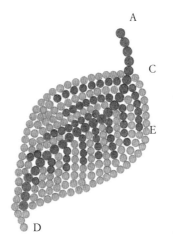

fig 1

81

blue poppy pillow

This design involves an effective combination of stitching and beading. Essentially, the background is stitched first and the beads added as an embellishment, accentuating the characteristics of the poppy flower. Some of the beads used here are Japanese in origin. Known as magatama beads, they have an off-center hole and will therefore hang at any angle allowing them to lie along the stitching.

Alternative finishes for the pillow might be the addition of a ready-made upholstery fringe or piping with a satin-biased edging, picking up on the color of the beads. Looped beaded tassels, finished with a bead drop in the corners might be attractive, too. All bead quantities given in this design are approximate.

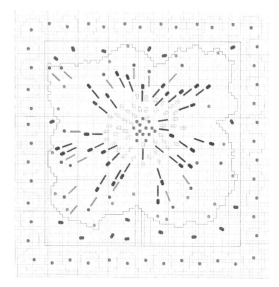

fig 1

You will need

12″ (30.5cm) square double-thread
    ecru canvas, 10 holes to 1″ (2.5cm)
Paternayan Persian yarn in colors
    shown on chart on page 84
Tapestry needle size 18 or 20
Sewing thread to match bead colors
Sewing needle
Small rectangular tapestry frame
    (optional)

59 3mm-diam green metallic beads
50 4mm-diam yellow glass beads
32 9mm-long lilac-purple bugles
25 lilac-purple magatamas
22 3mm-diam turquoise-blue
    metallic beads
17 4mm-diam cerise wooden beads
17 9mm-long pale turquoise bugles
15 large lilac-blue rocailles

To make

The finished needlepoint measures 8½″ (21 cm) square.

1 Fold canvas both horizontally and vertically, and sew a running stitch along both folds to find center point.

2 The needlepoint is worked using tent stitch (see page 78) and 2 strands of Persian yarn throughout. Each working length of yarn should be no more than 16″ (40cm). Start at center point and work the design outward, filling in the background last.

3 Using sewing thread and needle, stitch beads over surface of needlepoint following chart (fig 1). Sew bugles to radiate outward from center of poppy, following direction of petal veins. If not sewing each bead individually, it is best to make a fastening-off stitch before advancing on reverse side to next beading point.

NB If you have not used a frame to work the needlepoint, it may be necessary to stretch the finished work, following the instructions given here. It is essential to do this just before stitching the pillow cover together, as it may lose its shape again in about a day.

To stretch the finished work

1 Cover a clean board that is larger than the piece of work with a sheet of plastic and a piece of medium-weight cotton fabric. Be careful to check that the board is square: i.e. has 4 right-angled corners.

2 Spray needlepoint lightly with water, or dampen with a moist sponge. Place the top edge of the canvas parallel with the top edge of the board, right side facing upward.

3 Using tacks or nails and beginning in the center of the top edge of the unworked canvas, tack first to the left-hand side, and then to the right-hand side, with the tacks inserted at regular intervals of approx ¾″ (2cm).

4 Tack the bottom edge of the unworked canvas in the same way, using a draftman's triangle to check that the sides are at right angles to the top and bottom edges. Then tack left-hand side edge and right-hand side.

5 Lay board flat and allow the work to dry naturally. This may be several days. If the work is very distorted, it might be necessary to repeat the process to obtain a satisfactory finish.

520   353   302   543   553   554   620   632   771   772

beaded fruits

Beads and sequins are used here to add sparkle and extra definition to these fabric fruits. This technique works best on firmly woven fabrics, such as velvet, damask, or cotton chintz. To give added depth and richness of color, try using layers of different colored organza, echoing the bloom on the fruits themselves. Other fruits would also make attractive shapes for beading.

Strawberry

You will need

12" x 6" (30 x 15cm) red velvet
20" (50cm) silver-colored jewelry wire
Small pack polyester fiberfill
Small block beeswax
Tracing paper
Dressmaker's carbon paper
Sewing thread to match fabric
Beading or fine milliner's needle
120 2mm gold bugles
120 5mm-diam transparent iridescent pale gold cup sequins
100 apple-green rocailles
50 jade-green rocailles
5 pale green leaf-shaped beads

fig 1

fig 2

To make

1 Trace strawberry pattern on page 109 and cut out.
2 Pin pattern to wrong side of velvet, with a layer of carbon paper between pattern and fabric, taking care to follow grain line instruction. Mark opening and "pips," and cut out. Repeat twice more, to make 3 identical pattern pieces.
3 To sequin the strawberry, use pale gold cup sequins, with cup up, and gold cut bugles, and follow method described on page 79.
4 Pin fabric shapes wrong sides together and baste seams, leaving a 1¼" (3cm) opening at top edge for stuffing and to attach stem. Machine stitch, then clip seams at ¾" (2cm) intervals (fig 1).
5 Using a zigzag machine stitch, stitch raw edges to prevent them from unraveling, then turn right side out.

6 Stuff really tightly with polyester fiberfill. You might find it helpful to use the end of a pencil to push fiberfill into curves of strawberry if necessary. Turn under remaining seams and hand stitch them together, leaving a ⅜" (1cm) opening for stem.
7 For the stem, cut a 20" (50cm) length of silver-colored jewelry wire and fold over one end by about ¾" (2cm) to prevent beads from slipping off. Begin threading wire with a random mix of apple-green and jade-green rocailles. When you have threaded about 4" (10cm), bend wire over, thread another 4" (10cm) and twist this length around 1st 4" (10cm). Repeat this sequence, moving up and then down stem (fig 2). It is not necessary to cover all wire with beads for last 2 twists; some wire showing through will give stems a more delicate look.
8 Make sure there is an unbeaded length of wire left at end, and unbend ¾" (2cm) first turned over. Onto each of these 2 ends, thread a pale green leaf-shaped bead (fig 3), and secure by twisting ends together (fig 4).
9 Push completed stem into hole left in top of strawberry, then finish sewing seams together, passing thread through twisted wire a few times to secure stem.
10 Complete strawberry by sewing the other 3 green leaf shapes around base of stem below 1st 2 leaf-shape beads.

fig 3

fig 4

85

Pear

You will need

14" x 6" (35 x 15cm) lime-green glazed
  cotton chintz
12" (30cm) silver-colored jewelry
  wire
Small pack polyester fiberfill
Small block beeswax
Tracing paper
Dressmaker's carbon paper
Sewing thread to match fabric
Beading or fine milliner's needle
180 lime-green rocailles
180 5mm-diam transparent iridescent
  pale gold cup sequins
20 green rocailles
1 brown rocaille
1 8mm-diam copper cup sequin

To make

1 Trace pear pattern and 3 speckle mark
guides on page 109, and cut out
carefully on fabric.
2 Pin pattern to wrong side of chintz,
with a layer of carbon paper between
pattern and fabric, being careful to
follow grain line instruction. Mark
opening and speckles, and cut out.
Repeat twice more, to make 3 identical
pattern pieces. Next, again using carbon
paper, trace speckle marks from 3
pattern pieces to 3 fabric pieces.
3 To sequin the pear, use pale gold
sequins and lime-green rocailles and
follow method described on page 79.
4 Pin fabric shapes wrong sides together
and baste seams, leaving a ⅜" (1cm)
opening at top for inserting stem, and a
1½" (4cm) opening at bottom for
stuffing (see pattern). Machine stitch,
then clip seams at ¾" (2cm) intervals as
for strawberry.
5 Turn right side out. Stuff with
polyester fiberfill until a firm, really
tightly stuffed pear shape has been
formed. Use the end of a pencil to push
fiberfill into curves of pear if necessary.
Carefully turn under bottom seams and
hand stitch them together.
6 For the stem, cut a 12" (30cm) length
of silver-colored jewelry wire and fold
over one end by about ¾" (2cm) to

prevent beads from slipping off. Begin
threading wire with a random mix of
lime-green and green rocailles. When
you have threaded about 2" (5cm),
bend wire over, thread another 2"
(5cm) and twist this length around first
2" (5cm). Repeat this sequence, moving
up and then down stem as for
strawberry on previous page.

fig 1

7 Make sure there is an unbeaded length of wire at end, twist this around initial loop and then push completed stem into hole left in top of pear. Finish sewing seams together, passing thread through twisted wire a few times to secure stem, and finish by bending into a realistic pear stem.

8 Complete by stitching the copper cup sequin convex side outermost, anchored by the brown rocaille (fig 1).

Alternative finishes might involve using a fabric dye pen to create blemishes and bruises. You could also reduce the pattern pieces to make a branch of different sized pears, to be attached to a main stem, made using the method for the individual stalks.

cloche & mittens

A beautiful beaded triangle is the chief feature of this beaded cloche and mittens ensemble that evokes another age, a time when dressing to dine and dance was de rigueur. Knitting needles, yarn, and beautifully faceted crystal beads combine to capture the glamour of the 1920s. The charts accompanying the pattern indicate the bead threading sequence only, not the number of stitches and rows.

Used in combination with different yarns, cotton or silk perhaps, and appropriate beads, the beaded triangle could be repeated as an original edging for a blind, shelf, or a footstool, or used individually as a decorative feature to be applied to the neckline, shoulders, or the waist of garments.

Cloche

Gauge
28 sts to 2" (5cm) over single rib unstretched, using size 2 (2¾mm) knitting needles

Abbreviations
bd	bead
K	knit
lg	large
P	purl
pu	push up
psso	pass slipped st over
rem	remain(s)(ing)
rep	repeat
rnd(s)	round(s)
RS	right side
sl	slip purlwise
sm	small
st(s)	stitch(es)
sm	small
tog	together
WS	wrong side
yo	yarn over

You will need
Pair of size 2 (2¾mm) knitting
　needles for cloche rib and mittens
Set size 2 (2¾mm) double-pointed
　knitting needles for cloche crown
6oz (150g) ball 3-ply metallic
　knitting yarn
2 stitch holders
Large-eyed needle which will pass
　smoothly through all beads
For threading to knit cloche and mittens:
　435 small purplish-blue beads
　147 large purple faceted beads
　22 large pink faceted crystals
For triangles and mitten picots:
　414 small purplish-blue beads
For cloche crown:
　1 large purple faceted bead

For cloche triangle tassel:
　3 small purplish-blue beads
　2 large black rocailles
　2 small greeny blue beads
　1 large purple faceted bead
　1 large pink faceted crystal
　1 purple drop bead
For tassel strands:
　264 black cut rocailles
　96 greeny blue cut rocailles
　64 4mm amethyst bugles
　8 pink crystal rocailles
　8 8mm amethyst bugles
　8 6mm amethyst bugles
For mitten loops:
　78 garnet rocailles
　2 small purplish-blue beads
　2 large purple faceted beads

To make
Using size 2 (2¾mm) needles, cast on 194 sts and work single (K1, P1) ribbing for 5" (13cm).

Next row (RS) Slip 1 knitwise, K1, psso, K to last 2 sts, K2 tog. 192 sts rem. The first and last decreased sts of last row will form the ribbing seam.

Next row (WS) *K2 tog; repeat from *. 96 sts rem.

Cut off yarn. Transfer the rem 96 sts to three of the set of four double-pointed needles (31 sts on each needle).

Sew ribbing seam tog.

Set aside ribbing until it is needed again.

To thread beads for crown
Using large-eyed needle, thread beads onto ball of yarn, following bead sequence chart opposite (fig 1).

　Beginning at point A, read from right to left to point B and thread on a large purple faceted bead, a small purplish-blue bead, a large purple faceted bead, and so on as indicated.

　Move up to point B above this, and reading now from left to right to point C, thread on 7 large purple faceted beads as indicated.

　Continue reading from the chart and threading on beads in this way until you reach point U, smoothing beads gently

down yarn as you progress, so that you have about 12" (30cm) of yarn beyond the threaded beads at point U.

To make the crown
Using the end of the yarn beyond the threaded beads and gently sliding beads up as required, work the pattern in the round with RS (purl side) always facing as follows:

1st rnd (RS) P2, *sl 1, pu lg bd, P3, sl 1, pu sm bd, P3; rep from * 11 times more, ending last rep P1.

2nd, 4th, 6th, and 8th rnds Purl.

3rd rnd Using sm bds only, P2, *sl 1, pu bd, P3; rep from *.

5th rnd P2, *sl 1, pu sm bd, P3, sl 1, pu lg bd; rep from * 11 times more, ending last rep P1.

7th rnd As 3rd rnd.

9th rnd As first rnd.

10th rnd *P3, P2 tog, P6, P2 tog; rep from * to last 5 sts, ending P3, P2 tog. 81 sts.

11th, 13th, 15th, 17th, 21st, 23rd, and 25th rnds Purl.

12th rnd *P2 tog, yo; rep from * to last st, P1.

14th rnd As 12th rnd.

16th rnd P2 tog, *P2 tog, P3; rep from *, ending last rep P2. 64 sts.

18th rnd *P3, sl 1, pu lg bd, P3, sl 1, pu

sm bd; rep from * 7 times more.

20th rnd Using sm bds only, P1, *sl 1, pu sm bd, P3; rep from *, ending last rep P2.

22nd rnd *P3, sl 1, pu sm bd, P3, sl 1, pu lg bd; rep from * 7 times more.

24th rnd As 20th rnd.

26th rnd As 18th rnd.

27th rnd *P6, P2 tog; rep from * 7 times more. 56 sts.

28th rnd *P2 tog, yo; rep from *.

29th rnd Purl.

30th rnd As 28th rnd.

31st rnd *P5, P2 tog; rep from *. 48 sts.

32nd rnd Purl.

33rd, 35th, 37th, and 39th rnds Purl.

34th rnd *P3, sl 1, pu sm bd, P3, sl 1, pu lg bd; rep from * 5 times more.

36th rnd Using sm bds only, *P1, sl 1, pu bd; rep from * to last 2 sts, P2.

38th rnd *P3, sl 1, pu lg bd, P3, sl 1, pu sm bd; rep from * 5 times more.

40th rnd As 36th rnd.

41st rnd *P2, P2 tog; rep from *. 36 sts.

42nd rnd *P2, sl 1, pu lg bd, P2, sl 1, pu sm bd; rep from * 5 times more.

43rd rnd *P5, P2 tog; rep from * 5 times more. 30 sts.

44th rnd Using sm bds only, *sl 1, pu bd, P2; rep from * 9 times more.

45th rnd *P3, P2 tog; rep from * 5 times more. 24 sts.

46th rnd *P1, sl 1, pu lg bd, P1, sl 1, pu sm bd; rep from * 5 times more.

47th rnd *P2, P2 tog; rep from * 5 times more. 18 sts.

48th rnd *Sl 1, pu lg bd, P1; rep from * 8 times more.

49th rnd *P2, P2 tog; rep from * 3 times more, P2. 14 sts.

50th rnd *Sl 1, pu lg bd, P1; rep from * 6 times more.

51st rnd P3, (P2 tog, P1) twice, P2 tog, P3. 11 sts.

52nd rnd *Sl 1, pu sm bd, P1, sl 1, pu lg bd, P1; rep from * twice more, omitting P1 at end of last rep.

53rd rnd (P2 tog) 5 times, P1. 6 sts. Cut off yarn, leaving an end about 8" (20cm) long. Thread end through rem 6 sts. Pull the yarn tight and secure with a few stitches. Slip a large purple bead onto the yarn, sew it at the apex of the crown and weave in end neatly.

fig 1

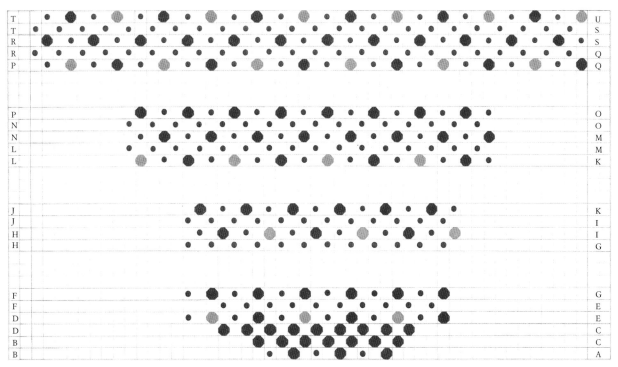

To thread beads for cloche triangle

The beaded triangle is made separately and sewn onto the cloche. Before casting on the sts, the beads should be threaded onto the yarn.

**Using large-eyed needle, thread beads onto ball of yarn, following bead sequence chart below (fig 2).

Beginning at point A, read from right to left to point B and thread on a small purplish-blue bead as indicated.

Move up to point B above this and, reading now from left to right to reach point C, thread on two small purplish-blue beads as indicated.

Move up to point C above this and, reading now from right to left to point D, thread on one small purplish-blue bead, one large pink faceted crystal and one small purplish-blue bead as indicated. Continue reading from chart and threading beads on to ball of yarn in this way until you reach point O, smoothing the beads gently down yarn as you progress so that you have about 12" (30cm) of yarn beyond the threaded beads at point O.**

To make the beaded triangle for cloche

Using size 2 (2¾mm) needles and the end of the yarn beyond the threaded beads, cast on 29 sts for the cloche triangle.

***Gently sliding beads up as required, work the pattern back and forth in rows as follows:

1st row K2, sl 1, pu sm bd, *K1, sl 1, pu sm bd, K1, sl 1, pu lg bd; rep from * 4 times more, (K1, sl 1, pu sm bd) twice, K2.

2nd row Knit.

3rd row K1, *K2 tog, yo; rep from * to last 2 sts, K2.

4th and 5th rows Repeat last 2 rows once more.

6th row Knit.

7th row K2, *sl 1, pu sm bd, K1, sl 1, pu lg bd, K1; rep from * 5 times more, sl 1, pu sm bd, K2.

8th row K2 tog, K1, *sl 1, pu sm bd, K1; rep from * 10 times more, sl 1, pu sm bd, K1, K2 tog.

9th row K2 tog, K1, *sl 1, pu sm bd, K1, sl 1, pu lg bd, K1; rep from * 4 times more, sl 1, pu sm bd, K1, K2 tog.

10th row K2 tog, K1, *sl 1, pu sm bd, K1; rep from * 8 times more, sl 1, pu sm bd, K1, K2 tog.

11th row K2 tog, K1, *sl 1, pu sm bd, K1, sl 1, pu lg bd, K1; rep from * 3 times more, sl 1, pu sm bd, K1, K2 tog.

12th row K2 tog, K1, *sl 1, pu sm bd, K1; rep from * 6 times more, sl 1, pu sm bd, K1, K2 tog.

13th row K2 tog, K1, *sl 1, pu sm bd, K1, sl 1, pu lg bd, K1; rep from * 2 times more, sl 1, pu sm bd, K1, K2 tog.

14th row K2 tog, K1, *sl 1, pu sm bd, K1; rep from * 4 times more, sl 1, pu sm bd , K1, K2 tog.

15th row K2 tog, K1, *sl 1, pu sm bd, K1, sl 1, pu lg bd, K1; rep from * once more, sl 1, pu sm bd, K1, K2 tog.

16th row K2 tog, K1, *sl 1, pu sm bd, K1; rep from * 2 times more, sl 1, pu sm bd, K1, K2 tog.

17th row K2 tog, K1, sl 1, pu sm bd, K1, sl 1, pu lg bd, K1, sl 1, pu sm bd, K1, K2 tog.

fig 2

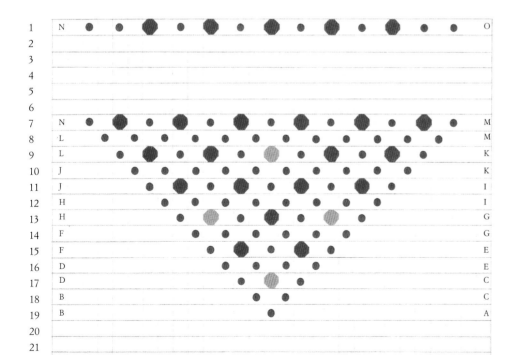

18th row K2 tog, K1, sl 1, pu sm bd, K1, sl 1, pu sm bd, K1, K2 tog.
19th row K2 tog, K1, sl 1, pu sm bd, K1, K2 tog.
20th row Knit.
21st row K2 tog, K1, K2 tog.
22nd row K3 tog.
Cut off yarn, leaving an end about 4in (10cm) long.

To fasten off the last st on the knitting needle, take yarn end through it, pull yarn tight, and weave end back into edge of work, before cutting it off neatly.***

With cloche ribbing seam at center back, position beaded triangle in center of left side of cloche ribbing and stitch it into last row of ribbing.

Mittens

To make
Using size 2 (2¾mm) needles, cast on 81 sts and work single (K1, P1) ribbing for 6" (16cm).
Next row Bind off first 26 sts, work in rib to last 26 sts, bind off rem sts. 29 sts rem on needle.

Cut off yarn and set sts aside until beads have been threaded onto yarn.

To thread beads for mitten triangle
Thread beads onto ball of yarn as for cloche triangle from ** to **.

To make beaded triangle for mitten
Using the yarn beyond the threaded beads, pick up 29 sts of mitten ribbing and using these sts, work beaded triangle for mitten as for beaded cloche triangle from *** to ***.

To finish
With right sides together, sew along first and last ribbing stitches to complete wrist ribbing. Starting at seam, sew a line of bead picots, as above for cloche, around cast-on edge of ribbing.

Starting again at seam of beaded triangle hand end, sew a similar line of picots, with a picot positioned on each side of triangle point. Attach a new thread to the point and thread on a

To finish
Using a strong thread and starting at one side of triangle, sew a continuous line of bead picots around V of triangle, using small purplish-blue beads. Make a fastening-off stitch and weave in thread ends invisibly.

To work the tassel
Work the tassel following the beading instructions on page 43.

Thread the 2 ends of thread at top of tassel into a needle and stitch into yarn at bottom point of triangle. Make one or 2 fastening-off stitches and pass needle down through top beads at top of tassel and cut off neatly. This completes the beaded cloche.

small purplish-blue bead, a large purple faceted bead, another small purplish-blue bead, and 39 garnet rocailles, which will form loop to slip over middle finger of your hand.

Check that 39 rocailles is neither too large nor too small and adjust number if necessary, always keeping an odd number of beads in loop, as this creates correct shape and protects the thread from wear (fig 3).

Bring needle back through last small purplish-blue bead to starting point. Fasten off neatly and insure that ends are woven in invisibly.
Make second mitten in same way.

fig 3

beaded denim shirt

This shirt represents a skilful combination of couched beading and appliqué. You could use it to add a unique accent to any plain fabric. It enables you to bring together fabrics, textures and colors in a way which would otherwise be difficult to achieve. Experiment further by beading a richly embellished satin appliqué motif, leaving more of the satin ground exposed, and applying this to a velvet evening jacket or throw.

You will need

Blue denim shirt
Fabric strong enough to support beaded motif (either with suitable printed motif, or to take transferred design)
Iron-on interfacing, if required
Needle fine enough to pass through beads twice when threaded
Sewing needle
Spool of matching polyester thread
Spool of matching sewing thread
Strong sewing thread
Tracing paper, dressmaker's carbon paper
Embroidery hoop or frame, large enough to contain complete motif
Rocailles (approximate quantities):
    760 dark green; 470 amber; 375 crimson; 325 scarlet; 275 gold; 245 dark amethyst; 185 leaf-green; 180 apple-green lined transparent; 170 brown; 140 pale pink rainbow; 130 crystal;100 cerise lined transparent
Round beads:
    2 6mm-diam pale green
    1 6mm-diam amber
Pearls:
    2 4mm-diam
    2 2mm-diam
    1 5mm-diam
    1 3mm-diam
Faceted crystals:
    16 2mm-diam pale green
    3 5mm-diam pale green
    3 3mm-diam amber
    2 6mm-diam pale green
    2 6mm-diam champagne
    2 6mm-diam amber
    1 5mm-diam amber
    1 3mm-diam pale green

To make

1 Cut a piece of your chosen fabric 18" x 14" (45 x 35cm), or larger if necessary to mount it in the embroidery hoop or frame. If fabric is light to medium weight, back with iron-on interfacing.
2 Trace fruit-bowl pattern on page 108, and using dressmaker's carbon, transfer it to center of wrong side of fabric.
3 Stitch around edge of pattern shape using zigzag stitch, to prevent it from unraveling when it is cut out after beading and to give a firm edge with which to appliqué beaded motif to shirt.
4 Mount prepared fabric right side up in embroidery hoop or frame, keeping warp and weft of fabric at right angles and fabric firmly stretched.
5 Thread 1 needle with approx 20" (50cm) polyester thread (for beads) and 1 with sewing thread. Referring to photograph on page 96, and using couching method detailed on page 80, begin by couching dark green stems of main leaves, and then leaves themselves. Complete fruits by beginning at outside edge and working couching inward. Thread on appropriate number, type and color of beads a short length at a time, and remember to pull both threads tightly while working.
6 For bunch of grapes, stitch down large beads and crystals singly first, then couch beads around them to fill in gaps between grapes. Then thread 6 or 7 small beads and stitch down to form arcs around large beads on top of couched background.
7 When beading is complete, cut carefully around zigzag stitching of pattern shape. Position beaded shape onto center of back of blue denim shirt and pin down carefully. Appliqué to shirt fabric by stitching with very small stitches through zigzag stitching, using strong sewing thread.

Patterns & designs

This chapter shows how to chart a design for beading, as well as giving lots of additional designs for many of the techniques and projects shown earlier in the book. There are alternative designs for bookmarks and pillow trimming, for bracelets and perfume bottles, for buttons and tassels. Patterns for fringes are also included, and there are decorative designs for pin-beaded baubles and wire-beaded creatures.

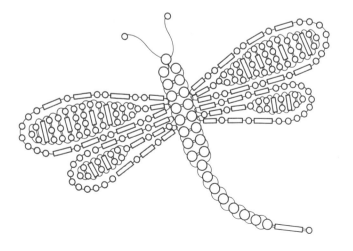

charting a design

When designing for beadwork, careful planning and drafting of a design is usually essential to ensure a perfect finished object. If you have ever left out a bead from a completed pattern you will appreciate how important accuracy is for the finished result.

You will need

A selection of graph paper to enable you to chart beads actual size

Tracing paper

Drafting ruler – a wide transparent ruler with a squared grid marked onto it

Graduated transparent circle template

Pair of compasses

Small draftman's triangle

Very fine 0.1 or 0.2 drafting pen

Sharpened pencil and eraser

Selection of fine point felt-tip pens and colored pencils to color-code beads

Charting designs

The beading technique determines the position of the beads in relation to each other. With needlewoven beading (fig 1, A), the beads hang between each other in alternate rows; with beaded fringe (fig 1, B), the beads are positioned on top of each other.

By practicing charting some basic design shapes for both these methods, you can see how they affect the shape. Use graph paper and a circle template with a fine pencil to chart some basic shapes (fig 2), using beads in between and on top of each other.

It is helpful to identify those designs that work well in a small scale, and those more effective in a larger scale before attempting to work them.

For example, in the leaf shape shown in fig 3, the smaller scale gives a crisper profile with beads worked on top of

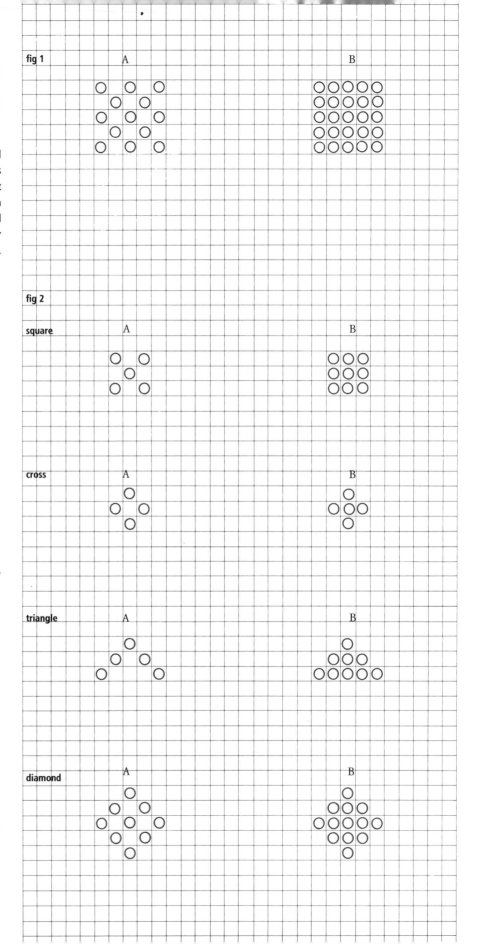

each other, rather than in between which results in a more blurred outline. A larger scale, however, gives a more effective result with beads threaded in-between each other. In general, because of the diagonal line possibilities of the in between beading, the technique lends itself to geometric, rather than linear or rounded designs, which are translated more effectively by beads being on top of each other. As with all techniques, there are always the "exceptions that break the rule," so experiment and use your own judgement. Practice drafting a variety of design shapes, either by drawing them onto the graph paper freehand, or by tracing designs and transferring them.

Color coding charted designs

Using the beads you have selected, match the colors as closely as possible to fine felt-tip pens or artists pencils. Where beads are difficult to match, choose an approximate color. If the charted design is small enough, it is helpful to do several extra drawings to experiment with varying the bead positions and the color balance. If the design is quite large or complicated, it might be best to make a photocopy of it to experiment.

Combining beads and bugles

Depending on the length of the bugles you are using, simply allow 2, 3, or 4 graph squares to represent them, as, for example, in the simple fringe pattern shown in fig 4.

Drafting repeats

By using a transparent drafting ruler, or by dividing the graph paper into blocks, you will be able to repeat the beaded design accurately. This is helpful for beaded fringe patterns. When you have decided on the design, make a key on the graph paper close to the charted design to indicate the bead shapes represented and a description of the different bead colors.

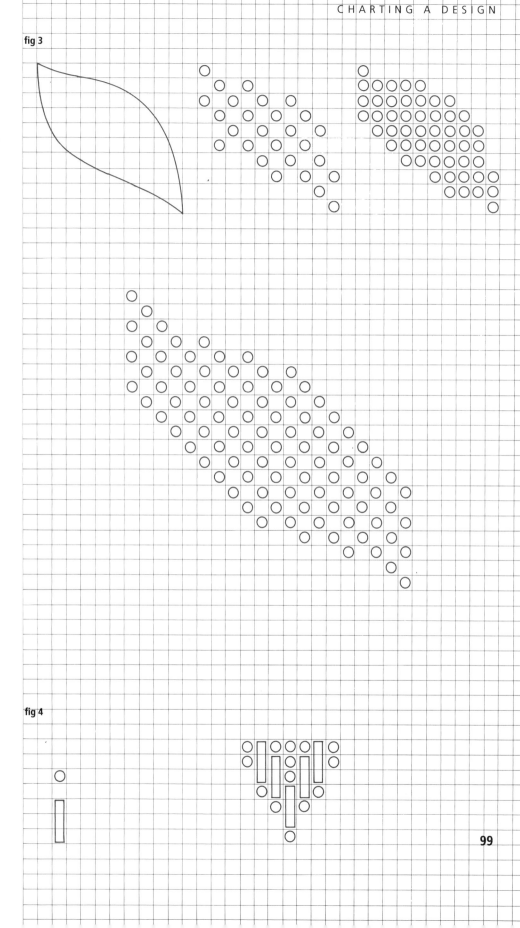

fig 3

fig 4

99

beaded bookmarks

Here are three variations on the theme of the needlewoven bookmark featured on page 15. The shaded beads are suggestions for varying colorways to emphasize the diagonal shapes that are naturally created by this technique. You can experiment by matching the beads to a variety of sumptuous ribbons, using watered silk, moiré, brocade, or satin. Accentuate the quality and finish of the chosen ribbon by using a combination of matt, chalk, metallic finish, or crystal beads. The final coup de grâce could be an extravagant drop bead. This simple beaded triangle is essentially a decorative trimming and could also be used repeated on a window shade or even a footstool edging.

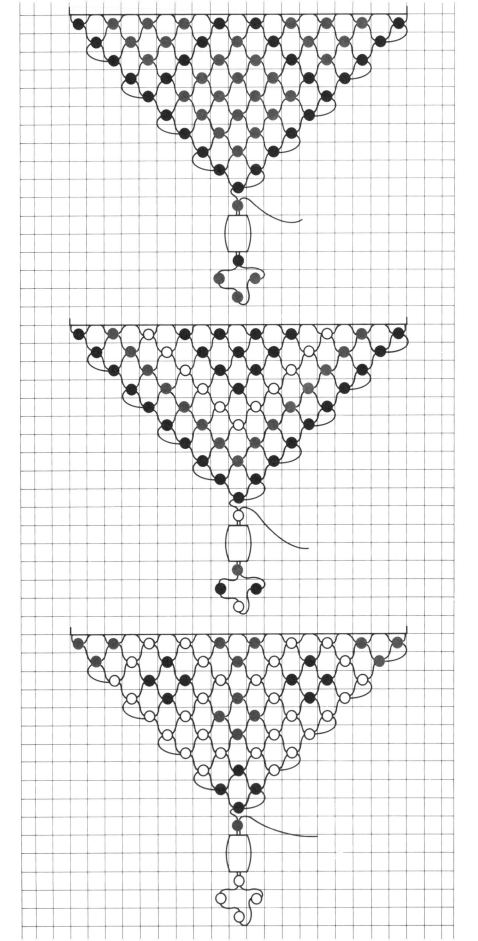

beaded trimmings

These are design alternatives to the edgings seen in the trimmed pillows on pages 16–21. Figs 1 and 2 involve one simple threading sequence. Figs 3 and 4 are slightly more complex, using two threading sequences. Fig 5 is the most intricate of all, with three bead threading sequences. These patterns would look lovely embellishing many soft furnishings, including decorative pillows, bolsters, curtains, or valances.

fig 1

fig 2

fig 3

fig 4

fig 5

101

bracelets

Beaded needlewoven strips, using rocaille or faceted beads, can be used to create bracelets, chokers, and belts with a traditional feel. In Victorian times black would often have been used, with highlights in gold, silver, or bronze beads. The 11-bead wide bands illustrated here give scope for many design possibilities as there is a "middle" bead (the 6th bead) that can facilitate various color and design possibilities. The completed beading can be further extended by an added picot of beads on each side (fig 2). The beaded fastenings can use special drops to add an extra touch of richness.

circular designs

These designs involve needlewoven beading, working in rounds rather than rows. The key to success is careful manipulation of the number of beads and the tension of the working thread. We have already seen this technique used to decorative effect in the perfume bottles on pages 32–37, but most three-dimensional forms can be embellished with this age-old beading tradition – from a candlestick holder to a parchment lampshade. The designs can be finished with a variety of lovely bead drops.

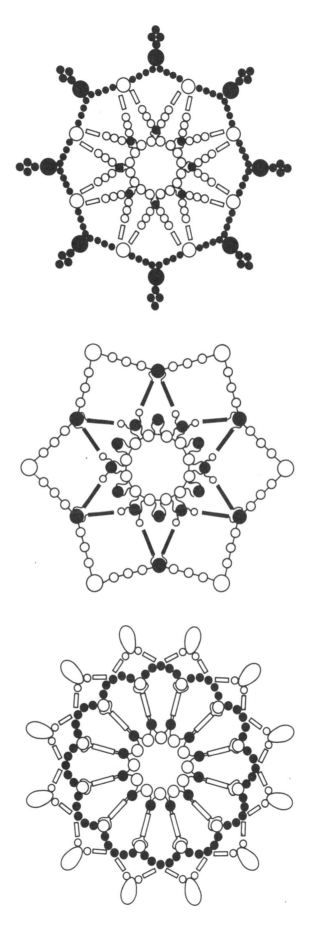

tassels & buttons

One of the most popular beaded finishes of all, beaded tassels can be used to complement numerous soft furnishings, as well as items of clothing and objets d'art. The technique for making a basic tassel is described on page 43. The range seen here would be particularly effective worked in silk and rayon threads, creating a shining resonance and lending luster to the finished work. Sequined buttons also make a lovely finish for soft furnishings. The final stylish touch could be a beautiful loc rosen bead at the button's center.

fringe patterns

The nature of beaded fringe – in particular, the close proximity of the bead strings – lends itself to intense, dramatic effects. Using the technique described on pages 56–57, you can experiment with color and shape. The shaded areas in figs 1 and 2 denote suggested colored bead areas: fig 3 has a pansy motif integrated as part of the design.

You can vary the finished shape of the fringe, ranging from a chevron finish (fig 1) to a wavy line (fig 2). Although the normal application of a fringe is usually over or in front of a light source, it can also be used to trim small bags or purses (see page 57).

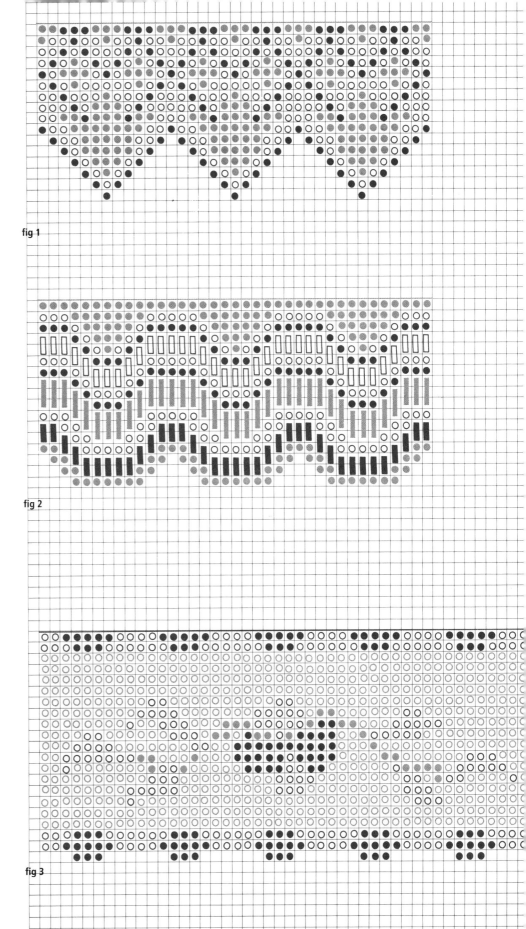

fig 1

fig 2

fig 3

- ⬤ purple rocaille
- ⬤ dark green rocaille
- ○ 2mm white cut bugle
- ○ background color

pin-beaded baubles

Decorative, fun, and festive, this collection of patterned baubles complements the designs seen on pages 68–71. For real sparkle, sequins and beads picked out in metallic shades and iridescent hues would be most effective. Simple figurative shapes or repeating geometric patterns work best.

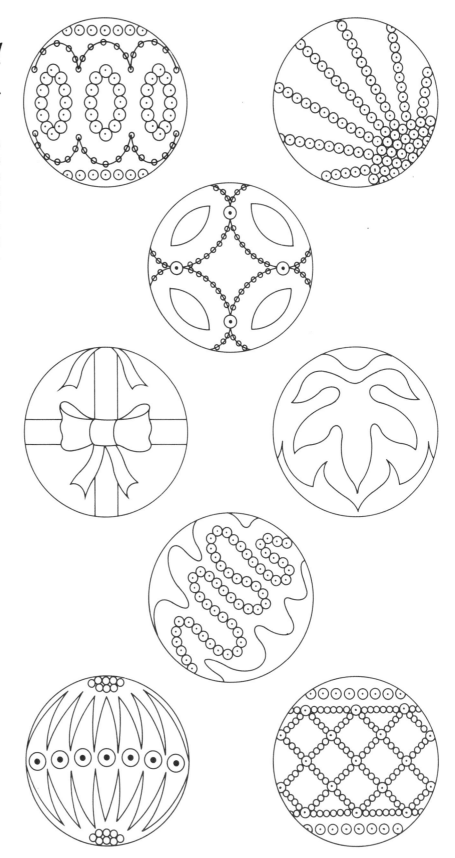

wire-beaded creatures

We have already seen wire-beading used to create beautiful beaded flowers and butterflies (see pages 72–75). Here are two delightful design alternatives. The dragonfly is made in two parts: body and wings. The enlarged detail shows how they are joined. The swift's head and body are made in one piece, worked from the beak downward. The enlarged detail illustrates how the tail feathers are attached. Its wings are joined following the instructions for the butterfly on page 74.

couched
fruit bowl

This reduced appliqué motif of a fruit bowl, spilling over with fruit embellished with couched beading, is positioned beneath the bottom of the yoke on the back of the denim shirt on page 94. It works very well on denim, but any firmly woven fabric would be appropriate.

1 square = ⅜″ (1 cm)

bowl and plate motif
couched beading

beaded fruits

The instructions for these embellished fruits, complete with pips represented by sequins, are on pages 85–87. The patterns here are actual size. If you wish to alter the size, you could trace the patterns onto graph paper to enlarge or reduce them, or use a photocopying machine. The pear has 3 speckle mark guides (numbered 1–3).

Other beaded fruit ideas might be a cherry, made from deep red satin and flat red sequins, or a blackberry made from satin or organza with purple, deep blue, and silver flat sequins.

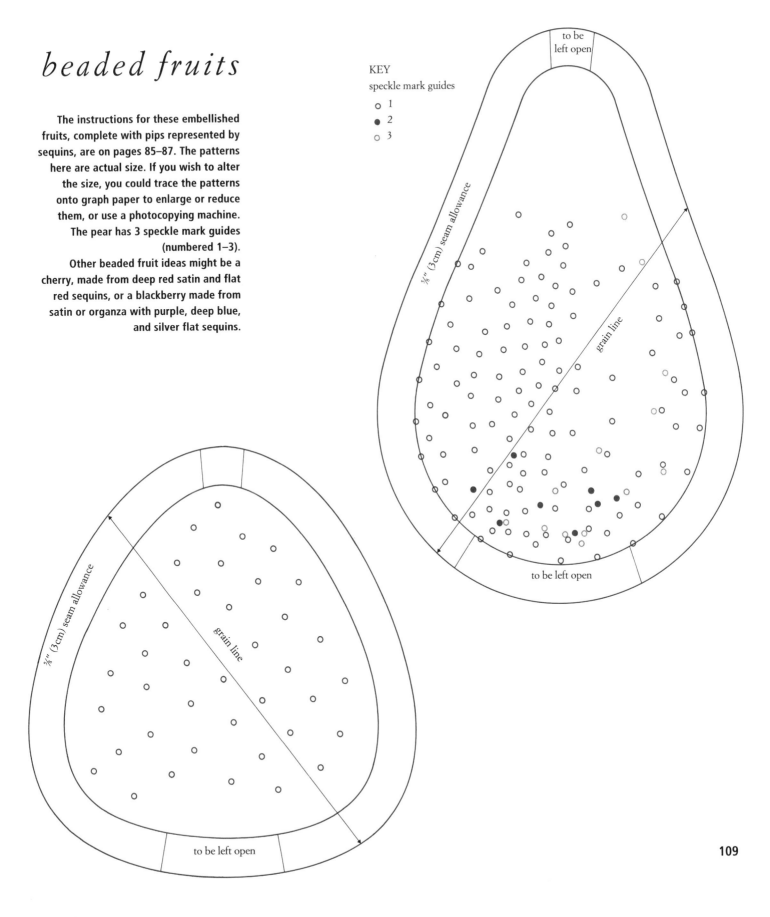

KEY
speckle mark guides

○ 1
● 2
○ 3

to be left open

⅛" (3cm) seam allowance

grain line

to be left open

⅛" (3cm) seam allowance

grain line

to be left open

index

acknowledgements

The author would like to thank the following: Alice Buck of Liberty Sewing School, Jenny Fitzgerald Bond of JLT Designs, and Mercedes Sosinowicz for their friendship, advice, and support.

Also for designing and making beautiful projects for the book and for their personal interest and encouragement, Candace Bahouth (Blue Poppy Pillow), Karen Spurgin (Lampshade Cover and Beaded Fruits), and Basia Zarzycka (Beaded Bolsters, Embellished Tassels, and Wire-beaded Flowers).

Thanks are also due to Mary Evans, Jane O'Shea, Carey Smith, Alison Shackleton, Tim Pearce, Vanessa Courtier, and all the rest of the excellent team at Quadrille who brought it all together and made it a happy experience, and to Linda Burgess for her exquisite photography.

I would also like to thank my mother and father, and Elaine and Haydon Luke, and especially Shaun Mullin, who has supported, encouraged and enabled me to develop my work over the past 25 years.

Last, but not least, J. C. Truelove for his endless support and patience, from this book's beginning to completion, and for still being there.

For the kind loan of beads for photography, the author and publisher would like to thank Ruth McCann and all at Ells & Farrier, and Karina Sterry at Hobby Horse.

Thanks are also due to pattern checker Marilyn Wilson.